SHORT FILM DISTRIBUTION

HOW TO MARKET YOUR SHORT FILM
SUCCESSFULLY. THE ESSENTIAL GUIDE TO
FESTIVALS, TV, VOD AND CO ...

DAVID M. LORENZ

CONTENTS

SHORT FILM DISTRIBUTION:

How to market your short film successfully. The essential guide to festivals, TV, VoD and Co ...

© 2020 - David M. Lorenz - Campfire Publications

To request permission, contact the publisher at

contact@davidmlorenz.com

First German paperback edition, November 2020

Third edition, January 2023

Cover Design: Abir Hasan

German version edited by: Sabrina Siemons

English version edited by: Kim Weller

YES, YOUR FILM WILL FIND AN AUDIENCE!

Nowadays, there are more possibilities than ever to distribute a short film. Thanks to the Internet, you can send it to the remotest corners of the world with just a few clicks. Several film festivals show short films. Almost every city has one. And who knows, with a little luck you might win a prize. Or you might succeed in getting your film into distribution. You might be able to sell it to a TV station, or you might be able to recoup part of the production costs (maybe even more) via video-on-demand providers. And with a bit of effort, your film might be seen by a large audience on an online platform. It may even find an audience of millions!

We are living in the best time when it comes to reaching other people worldwide. I know from experience that there is an audience somewhere for even the weirdest and most absurd films. But the question is how you find this audience. And this is precisely what I will explain to you step by step in the following pages.

WHAT IS NOT TAUGHT IN ANY FILM SCHOOL

I made my first short film at the age of seven - a very ketchup-heavy horror flick. I still remember exactly how I presented it to my family. Everyone was sitting in front of the old tube television, attentive and captivated by the moment. I was extremely excited and noticed every movement of my audience. Pure goosebumps. Long after the polite applause had died down, I was the proudest child *ever*.

As a result, I spent my school time making more films. A few classmates and I established a "production company", and we shot one action movie after the other. As soon as a film was finished, we booked a room in our city's art-house cinema and invited the whole school. The house was always full. When we turned the projector on, I peeked out from behind the curtain and watched how enthralled everyone was by what we had captured on mini-DV. At the exit, we collected money to finance the next film. But most of all, we collected compliments. I was high, and filmmaking became my drug. As a rather introverted boy, I had finally found my way of expression.

After school, I started working in the film industry in Munich, Sydney, Vienna, and Berlin and finally studied film. Everywhere I went in my career, I made more short films.

But there was a problem: I found information everywhere about making movies, but rarely about how to ensure they would be seen. So I had to find out a lot on my own. This learning process took me several years. I made mistakes and missed some chances; but little by little, I developed several distribution strategies, and the audience grew.

In the meantime, my films have travelled to more than 80 countries and been shown at over 800 film and music festivals, as well as at art exhibitions, in aeroplanes, in forests, on mountain peaks, and even in a research station in Antarctica. I have won more than 60 film awards and have been able to sell my films to some television stations.

Today I work for one of the biggest short film agencies worldwide. This allows me to exchange ideas with the organizers of over 7,000 film festivals, and we have distributed a large number of films that have been shown at festivals such as Clermont-Ferrand, Cannes, Berlinale, Sundance, Venice, Locarno, Toronto, Tribeca, Shanghai, Palm Springs, and many others. I was a part of festival juries worldwide and gave workshops on short filmmaking and short film marketing.

I want to pass on my collected knowledge in the following chapters and explain how to market a short film properly. I want to help you be seen and heard. For this reason, I have written a guide on short film distribution, which I would have liked having myself in the past. After reading this book, you will know how to distribute your short film successfully, whether it is documentary, fictional, experimental, or animated.

After that, it is up to you which of this advice you follow. I would suggest you treat them as recipes. Feel free to add more salt or pepper here and there or to reinterpret them entirely. However, if you haven't yet marketed a film, I advise you to follow my advice more strictly, as it has been proven a thousand times over.

So, the work has been done for you! This book summarizes the knowledge that I lacked when I started out. It is full of proven principles and practical basics; you just have to read it carefully and then act.

THE NEVER-ENDING STORY

The film industry is, more than ever before, subject to rapid change. This also applies to film distribution. New online offers and companies appear almost daily, while others disappear again. So, it is challenging to be always one hundred per cent up to date.

In this book, I mention many online services and resources. The last time I checked the corresponding internet addresses was in January 2023. Furthermore, I cannot guarantee the existence or content of the linked pages in the short term. But I have written this book with great care, and am keen to keep it up to date. Therefore, I would appreciate having feedback from you. If you have discovered discrepancies or information that is no longer up to date, please send me a short e-mail at contact@davidmlorenz.com.

Would you like more information on a specific subject? Did reading the book leave open questions about short film distribution? Then write to me! I will try to help you as soon as possible.

Ideas or suggestions that make it into the next edition of this book are mentioned in the acknowledgements; of course, only with your permission. You will also receive an updated version.

However, kindly note that I am not a lawyer, and this is not legal, contractual, or financial advice. This is my opinion, and I cannot answer any legal, contractual, or financial questions.

I cordially invite you to use content and thoughts from this book for your purposes and projects. Then I would be grateful if you do not forget me in these and mention me by name. If you intend to copy more than one paragraph, I hereby ask that you obtain my prior consent.

Now a short and concluding commentary on language rules. I know the rules of grammar, and I like them. But I also like to start sentences with an AND or an ABOUT, end them with prepositions and create new words, among other things--because I feel that this keeps everything informal and immediate. I hope you will forgive me here!

PART I

PREPARATION

You shed blood, sweat, and tears and finally made your short film. You showed it to your family, fellow students, colleagues, or friends, and you got a pat on the back. Now you want to present your masterpiece to the whole world as soon as possible. I can understand that. But before you rush into marketing, you'd better pause for a moment and ask yourself a crucial question: Is the film *really* finished?

1

IS THE FILM REALLY FINISHED?

To carry out a serious distribution of your short film - no matter in which form - it is essential to change it as little as possible from now on. Preferably not at all.

For example, if you're still thinking about shooting an alternate ending, shortening a scene, or re-recording dialogue, it's too early to start marketing. In that case, you should instead go back to the film set or the editing room and finish the work.

The short film distribution starts by sending it to select, renowned film festivals to enable an appropriate national and international premiere for your work. However, these festivals receive several thousand submissions each year, and usually, it is not possible to submit the same film a second time. So, you only have a tiny chance to get it accepted. Please don't waste it by sending imperfect films! Before submitting your work to Cannes, you should be 99% convinced that what you are uploading is the final version, the *real* final cut.

I also strongly advise against submitting films where the colour correction or sound design hasn't been completed yet. Sure, you can enclose a note stating that these things will be done before the start of the festival. But even if you can assume that the curators can abstract, such a procedure will diminish the overall impression they will have of your film.

Especially at more prominent festivals, there is often a less trained group of volunteers, usually students, who make a pre-selection to save the final decision-makers' time and headaches. Often, this group's ability to abstract is much smaller than that of the actual curators because they lack experience. It can happen that people quickly click to the next film because the sound is too exhausting, the look of the film is irritating, or it makes an unprofessional impression in some other way.

Therefore, take the time you need and complete your work before taking any further steps. Do not let festival deadlines upset you. In the meantime, there are many top-class film festivals at which to give your short film a great start. The calendar is full of exciting festivals. If you missed Cannes, the world will not end. Especially since a year passes quickly and you can try your luck again soon, if another attractive promise hasn't arrived by then.

So once again: Is your film finished? Is the current version the optimum of what could be achieved in the post-production under the given circumstances?

If you check the Yes box → then browse further.

If you check the No box → then close the book and go back to the editing room.

Okay, there is a third option. Of course, it is possible that - contrary to what I've said - you decide to submit a film that is not 100% finished because you want to meet a particular deadline, for example. I don't think this is a good idea, but I don't want to say that it is impossible. If you decide to do so, you should place a title card at the beginning of the screener that clearly and concisely describes what you are still working on. That way the curators know that the annoying background noise is not a failed artistic expression, but that you just haven't had time to clean it up yet.

TIP: Festivals usually cannot update your submission after you have made a change. This means that in most cases, the decision will be based on the version you submitted first. However, there is a practical loophole here: If you use a link to Vimeo for your submissions, you can update your film yourself without the festivals noticing. With Vimeo, you have the option of overwriting the old version of your film with a new one without changing the created viewing link. However, you should be extremely careful with each of these overwrites and make sure that you overwrite your film and do not generate a new link. And in any case, you must be very careful not to delete a film link that you have already sent to other festivals. This is important. Once you start using a film link for submissions, it should be kept for a longer period (at least three years).

THE PERFECT PREVIEW SCREENER

Okay, you've decided that your movie is ready. Then you should export a version that is ready to be sent to festivals.

Forwarding a film was quite complicated until a few years ago. I still remember burning lots of DVDs and spending all my money on stamps. The colleagues of the generation before me can probably only smile tiredly about this since they had to send Digibeta cassettes or even film copies weighing several kilograms. But that is history. Nowadays, films are sent online, with a few simple steps, via a streaming link.

In the professional short film sector, Vimeo has established itself as the most widely used platform. Since there are a few things to consider with this provider (despite all its simplicity), let's take a quick look at Vimeo.

But again, a step back. Firstly, of course, you must export your film. That is, generate a version that can be used for viewing. In general, I would advise you to export a file of high quality, at least with HD resolution.

Vimeo accepts most codecs but recommends using H.264 for best results. To maintain maximum control over the video quality, I recommend you upload an MP4 file (H.264 codec) with a resolution of 1080p. The frame rate should lie between 24 fps and 30 fps and the bit rate between 10,000 kbps and 20,000 kbps. Also make sure that the sound is exported with the ACC-LC codec, with a data rate of 320 KBS and a sampling rate of 48 kHz.

IMPORTANT! After uploading, you should check that everything is played back correctly and in high quality, because Vimeo will convert the file again. In most cases, the quality is still perfect, but errors may occur. Therefore, be sure to watch the movie in full length after you have uploaded it.

DOES YOUR FILM NEED A WATERMARK?

You have probably seen a bootleg of a Hollywood blockbuster with a digital watermark. These copyright symbols are intended to prevent films from being copied without permission. They usually take the form of company logos or texts and are placed semi-transparently over the image. This may be justified in the feature film sector, where illegal online publication can cause significant financial damage. Therefore, production companies and other institutions are keen to find the culprits.

In the short film sector, however, such measures are unusual and sometimes even frowned upon. I would therefore advise against integrating visible watermarks such as a festival copy or preview screener. This merely distracts the curators. Pirate copies of short films are still extremely rare. And if it happens, branding won't help you either, because professionals can quickly and effortlessly remove these marks. I would even go so far as to say that a digital watermark in the short film sector creates a rather unprofessional impression. In summary: You can save yourself the effort and time.

However, if you still want to mark your film, please keep the watermarks as small and unobtrusive as possible, because they simply interfere with the viewing of the film.

4
———

THE MOST IMPORTANT VIMEO SETTINGS

A fter you have finished exporting the film, you should upload it to Vimeo next. In the following paragraphs, I will give you a few tips on making the most out of the platform's potential and which settings you should pay attention to so that you avoid problems later in the distribution.

1.) The Password. You have to create a password so that not everyone can watch or download your film, but only the group of people you choose. It is best to choose a simple password for the movie links. This way, there is a high chance that everyone who gets the link to your movie will see it and not encounter password transfer errors instead.

2.) The Download Function. You should activate the download function.

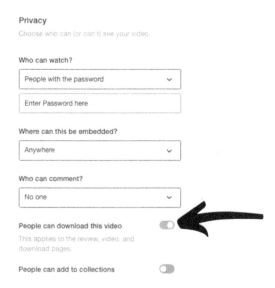

This means that you enable the viewer to download the short film using the link and password provided. That step is essential because many festivals want to download the films before they view them. Most curators like to do this to judge your film in peace, without annoying interruptions caused by loading problems. Do them a favour and activate this function. It will pay off.

As you have noticed, it is not advisable to be too hasty or careful here. Especially since not activating this function does not make it impossible to download your movie anyway. There are many programs or simple browser extensions that make this possible within a few clicks. You don't have to be a hacker to do this. So, there is no value in activating this function. It would only make it more difficult for some festivals to view your film.

3.) The Embedding Function. It is also crucial that you agree to the embedding of your video.

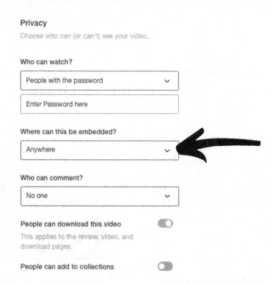

After this checkmark has been set, it is possible to integrate the video into other websites and portals; only this way, festivals can view it within the submission platforms without it being forwarded to Vimeo. This checkmark is essential for all forms of festival submissions. In any case, your film remains password protected.

4.) Further Information. Under your film, you can publish additional information about the project. You can use this for advertising.

For example, if the film has been shown at renowned festivals or won a few prizes, you can promote it here. Likewise, a well-written logline that arouses curiosity could have its effect here. Or, if famous actors appear in the film, you could point it out in this window.

However, with this information, you are walking a fine line between advertising and bragging. I would, therefore, not overdo it but only insert the most meaningful information. In the end, curators don't like their opinions to be influenced too openly.

Also, be aware that not everyone watching the movie will see this information, especially if you embed it in submission platforms; usually only the video itself will be forwarded.

5.) The Subtitles. Within Vimeo, you have the excellent opportunity to include various subtitles, which the viewer can choose from.

You should use this option if you already have subtitles in different languages. If not, don't worry. Festivals often offer their subtitles in the respective national language, and you will most likely receive subtitles in various languages during the film's festival career.

What you need are English subtitles if the language in your movie is different from English. The subtitles should either be integrated directly into the film or be available through Vimeo.

Because there is, unfortunately, a lot of confusion around subtitles, especially around their design, I have dedicated a short chapter to them.

5

ABOUT THE ART OF SUBTITLING

I f your film is not in English, you must subtitle it in English. You should be careful about this. Poorly translated or misplaced subtitles have the potential to destroy the impact of your film on the audience. They can quickly become very distracting and annoying. So, it's best to make sure you have proper subtitling from the beginning, in order for the audience to immerse themselves in your film.

Ideally, you have subtitles in different languages. It would be perfect if they were available to you in the form of a PDF and especially as an SRT file. You can then easily integrate them into your video using Vimeo, as described in the previous chapter. Besides that, film festivals occasionally ask for subtitle lists to create their subtitles. SRT files are also the most popular.

It is not necessary to be creative when creating subtitles. They don't need to be coloured in turquoise (or yellow) or set in the font of the month. There are clear industry standards (yes, horrible thought) that have proven themselves a thousand times over—here is no need to reinvent the wheel here.

On the contrary, every deviation from the standard irritates the audience and distracts from the film.

For the screener, the easiest way to add subtitles is to use the corresponding option in Vimeo. This allows the viewer to decide for himself whether he needs them or not. Nonetheless, you also have the option to burn the subtitles directly into the video, as you probably will with most screening copies.

To avoid the subtitles attracting too much attention and distracting from the movie, you should make sure that:

1.) They are readable. It is best to use a standard sans-serif font like Arial, Tahoma, or Verdana, in about 36pt, in white (or a very light grey), with a thin black border and a subtle drop shadow. The eye is so accustomed to these fonts that they are quick to grasp.

A font that is also increasingly used for subtitles is Roboto Medium. It is used by default on YouTube, for example. You can see that you still have a choice here, despite everything. But whichever font you choose, please avoid very thin or too thick strokes.

The subtitles should also be positioned in the lower part of the screen - a maximum of two lines of text per insertion. Try to keep them short. Preferably no more than 36 characters per line. And if two lines are inserted, they should both be about the same length.

2.) They are correct. Spelling or grammar errors are more than irritating to many viewers. Therefore, it is best to make sure that a native English speaker has checked the subtitles. If you don't know anybody, you still can hire a translator. You can quickly find someone qualified on online platforms for freelancers such as Fiverr.com, Upwork.com, or Textbroker.-

com. This can also be surprisingly inexpensive, since it's about a few subtitles and not about long texts such as in a novel.

3.) They are long enough to be seen. Nothing is more tiresome in foreign-language films than subtitles that disappear before you have had a chance to read them. But reading usually takes more time than listening. Therefore, it may be necessary to see the subtitles for a longer time. This sometimes leads to them being faded out a while after the protagonists have finished speaking. But this is entirely legitimate and often the rule. The main goal is that the audience can follow the action. A rule of thumb: If you, as a director or editor, have the time to read the subtitles twice in a row, then the viewers who are watching the film for the first time should also have enough time to grasp them once.

WARNING! Don't overdo it. You shouldn't forget that the audience came mainly to see pictures. Also, give them the time to look up from the subtitles and enjoy the film.

4.) They are short. As just explained, the viewer must have enough time to read the subtitles. You can achieve this by showing them longer. But you can also adapt the sentences yourself. Do not be afraid to shorten or simplify them a little. It is common practice that subtitles are often used with a more straightforward vocabulary; that the syntax is sometimes changed, or that parts of sentences are reformulated and summarized. Use the available leeway, but make sure that the essence of the text is not changed.

5.) They are synchronous. Because humans hear faster than they read, subtitling is always a kind of walk on a tightrope. On the one hand, you should be concerned that all dialogues reach the viewer. On the other hand, they should also be reasonably lip-synchronized. If the dialogues are too far away from what is reproduced in the subtitles, the viewer instinctively feels it. This can be very irritating. That's why a bit of sensitivity is required when setting subtitles.

* * *

TIP: If this task is too much for you or you don't have enough time for it, it may make sense to hire a professional. Several subtitling companies work with native speakers and can help you in the shortest possible time.

* * *

IF YOU WANT to delve even deeper into the world of subtitles, I can recommend the phenomenally detailed guide by Dr. Karamitroglou, who is a member of the European Association for Studies in Screen Translation (ESIST) and the British Institute of Translation and Interpreting (ITI): https://translationjournal.net/journal/04stndrd.htm.

And the extensive recommendations of the BBC are also interesting in this context: https://Bbc.github.io/subtitle-guidelines.

6

THE ADDITIONAL MATERIAL THAT MAKES YOUR FILM A SUCCESS

O kay, you have decided that your movie is finished and uploaded a screener with English subtitles to Vimeo. Congratulations! The crucial first step has been taken. Now we can get started.

It's time to gather the additional materials you need for almost every step you take next. The overall goal here is to make a potential audience as curious as possible. It's all about presenting your project in the best possible light; right, it's all about advertising.

I have divided the additional materials you need for a successful distribution into two groups. The first checklist contains essential things. You will need these for all further steps and as soon as possible. In the second list are the things that will become important a little later. In addition to this short, arranged checklist, I will explain in detail what the headwords stand for.

I know, it can be challenging to put these materials together. But at this point, it is definitely worth the effort, because the same materials are needed again and again for all further steps in the distribution. If you collect them conscientiously now, you will save a lot of time and energy in the future. And the chances that your film will be seen will increase immensely.

CHECKLIST ADDITIONAL MATERIAL

ESSENTIAL

- 3-5 film stills
- logline
- synopsis
- director's photo
- biography and filmography of the director
- press kit

ADVANCED

- poster of the film
- director's statement
- subtitles in other languages
- cast and crew list
- trailer
- web page (or social media page)
- biography and filmography of other team members
- making of (photos and/or video)

* * *

TIP: I would highly recommend storing this material clearly labelled and in a cloud of your choice. Then you can access it from anywhere and, above all, forward the files with just a few clicks.

Over the years, the following classification of the folders has proven to be very useful for me.

I have a main folder, which already contains the essential information about the film in its folder title, such as the film's title, running time, year of production, and production country. This looks as follows, for example:

SORRY_TO_INTERRUPT_
Germany_10_Min_2020

This folder contains the following subfolders:

01_Press Kit / 02_Stills / 03_Poster / 04_Foto_Director / 05_Dialogue_List / 06_Other

All information should be in English, since we are interested in the international marketing of the film.

If you use Dropbox (like me in this example), you can copy the download link with just one right click and quickly forward all materials (or only parts of them). This comes in very handy because you will be asked about these things very often.

* * *

7

LOGLINE, SYNOPSIS AND FILM STILLS

A few film stills, a logline, and a short synopsis are essential for any form of distribution. This is the absolute minimum of additional material you need before you can go on to any further steps.

On the one hand, these materials should make a potential audience as curious as possible; and on the other, they should give a great first impression of your film. They will appear in the programs of festivals, broadcasters, or online platforms, for example. In most cases, the logline and film stills are all people see before deciding which film they will watch. They, therefore, have a fundamental impact on the success of your film. That's why I'm going to say a few more words about them below.

Film Stills

With the film stills, you can promote your film. They have to rock. Therefore, choose the most expressive ones. If there was a still photographer on location, perfect—if not, export a few stills from your editing timeline. Or create screenshots. This is quite common in the short film world.

On the one hand, the film stills should have a sufficiently high resolution to be integrated into websites and printed in program booklets. On the other hand, you should make sure that the file sizes do not get too big, because they must be sent and uploaded very often.

JPEG or TIF files with around 300 dpi and file sizes of less than 3 MB each should be sufficient for all distribution purposes. Ideally, you should also have the same stills in a lower resolution and especially under 1 MB.

Make sure that the film title is included in the name of the stills to avoid unpleasant surprises. I have often seen festival brochures, in which the images were accidentally mixed up. If you name them clearly, you have at least done your part to prevent such a mishap.

It is best to number the stills according to your personal preference. Often only one picture can be printed in festival catalogues and usually the first best one is taken. Put the numbering at the end of the file name. Festivals often must assign hundreds of stills, and it is merely most helpful if the file name begins with the film title and not with a number.

It is also important to mention the rights holder. Speak to the person who owns the copyright to the picture. That is usually the still photographer or the cinematographer. This information is usually published by the festivals.

In summary, a proper designation should contain the following information:

"Title_of_the_film"_Cby_"Name of the copyright holder"_"Ranking number".jpeg

It would look like this, for example:

Sorry_to_Interrupt_Cby_Erika_Still_01.jpeg

If you name your pictures accordingly, you will spare the nerves of some volunteers and interns. Besides that, the chance that you will experience a nasty surprise is reduced.

Logline

Next, you need a gripping logline, a one-liner that summarizes your film's plot as concisely and catchy as possible. It's best to ask yourself a few questions:

What is at stake? How can you describe the essence of the film in one sentence? How would you summarize the plot if you only had 10 seconds to do so? What is the shortest possible pitch?

Maybe you also have the logline at hand with which you advertised your project in pre-production? Or do you remember what you answered when you were asked what your film was about?

But even in this case, it is worth thinking again and checking how helpful this logline will be in marketing the film, and whether it will still do justice to it after the shooting and editing.

Writing an effective and meaningful logline is an art that entire books have been written about. It can be a great challenge, and you may need a few tries before you get something satisfying on paper. However, the logline is an essential key to the successful distribution of the film.

To spur your creativity a little, I collected a few loglines of well-known short films:

1) "A lovestruck darts champion finds his prayers are answered -- literally -- when he mysteriously receives a box of love-inducing darts."

2) "On his way to the polls, an idealistic yet absent-minded voter has to endure continuous waves of racist cab drivers and their offensive remarks."

3) "A German mother lies to her son about where the Nazis are sending their Jewish neighbours to."

4) "A noisy neighbour, a drug dealer, and an angry husband make for a move-in day that two men will never forget."

5) "While a young black man is harassed on a streetcar by an older woman, the other passengers remain silent."

6) "Having reached the lowest point in his life, a self-destructive man on the brink of demise receives an unexpected call from his estranged sister to be the curfew for her young daughter for the night."

It may well be that one or the other of these one-liners looks familiar to you. Each of these short films was successful and won an Oscar. Those were the titles:

1) God of Love (2010)

2) Election Night (1998)

3) Toyland (2007)

4) The New Tenants (2009)

5) Black Rider (1993)

6) The Curfew (2012)

It is best to write down several loglines directly now. Brainstorm until you have one that has the potential to make the reader curious. Do not overthink here—just scribble things down. It's best not to read on until you have written down five to ten possible loglines.

WARNING! Do not confuse the logline with the so-called tagline. A logline summarizes in one sentence what your movie is about. A tagline is a short, imaginative saying or slogan that arouses the reader's emotions and curiosity without necessarily summarizing the content of the film.

For example, a famous tagline reads: "EARTH - take a good look. Today could be your last". Well, which film is it? Right, it's a film by Roland Emmerich. If it's Independence Day, the logline for this blockbuster could then be as follows: Aliens try to destroy Earth on Independence Day.

In other words, the logline appears in the festival or television program, while the tagline is printed on the film poster.

Logline Checklist

Do you have a logline that seems appropriate for your film now? Then recheck it according to the following criteria:

• **Do not use character names.** When describing the protagonists, refer to their role in the script instead. For example, write about the teacher, father, homeless person, etc.

• **Describe the protagonists** with one or two strongly characterizing words, so that every reader has a picture directly in front of them. The lonely writer. The ambitious but emaciated banker. The daydreaming teenager, etc.

• **Raise the stakes.** Is the reader immediately aware of the challenges your protagonist must face? Can you put the hurdles he has to overcome more forcefully into words? Is it possible to formulate them in a more worrying or threatening way?

• **Every word must fit.** You only have one sentence to describe your film. Do not waste letters. Check all the words used and cross out those that turn out to be unnecessary.

• **Include the genre.** Does the reader get a feeling for the style of the film? Can he estimate whether it is a comedy or a drama? In a winning logline, the tone of the film and the genre should shine through.

• **Tip for advanced users:** Try to add a dash of irony. Loglines in which the character and the situation contradict each other are usually the most interesting.

Black Snyder describes this concept in his famous guide for screenwriters:

"The fix of an idea that doesn't grab me - comedy or drama - almost always is to find the 'irony' of it. What gets our attention, what is the 'hook,' the 'sizzle' of an idea? What's 'ironic' about Erin Brockovich is not the plot, which finds a crusader exposing the wrongs of a powerful company, but the fact that the person doing the crusading is the very last person on Earth who would be called to this duty. The irony is not only the 'sizzle,' it hints at the transformation of the hero, and the size of the challenge as well."

A lawyer who cannot lie. A time manager who is stuck on an island with all the time in the world. A king who cannot speak to his people. These are ironic conflicts that arouse interest in the reader.

• **Break the rules.** Feel free to ignore the points above, especially if your film is an experimental film. All these are principles, not strict rules. In the end, it's only important that the reader of the logline gets curious about your film and gets an idea of what it is all about.

Synopsis

Next, you need a summary of your film. It should be as short and concise as possible. The priority is to make the reader curious.

The synopsis is based on the logline and gives a little more information. You should answer the following questions in one paragraph (3-5 sentences):

• Who is the protagonist of the film? What does he look like?

• Where and how does it all begin? Describe the initial situation briefly.

• What is the goal of the protagonist? What does he want?

• What does the protagonist have to fight on the way there, or what stands in his way?

You can also start the synopsis with the logline and then get more detailed. That could look like this, for example:

"Two orphan brothers, 16 and 9 years of age struggle through life in the streets of Mexico City. For their dream of a better future, they put aside every peso they make.

When the older one falls in love and uses their money to take a girl out, the younger one finds out about the betrayal and takes off for good. Twenty-five years later they meet again ..."

This is the synopsis of "Quiero Ser" (2000), an enchanting short film by Florian Gallenberger.

* * *

WARNING! Writing a gripping synopsis can be a tightrope walk. On the one hand, you should provide more information to make the reader even more curious about the film. On the other hand, you shouldn't reveal too much, because that could reduce the interest. In other words: You should never spoil too much in the synopsis.

* * *

IT IS best to keep this summary under 300 characters. Especially in the short film sector, there is often no room for excessive text in the program booklets. So, if you don't want your synopsis to be mutilated by someone else, keep it as crisp as possible yourself.

Film festivals are happy if they can conveniently take a logline and synopsis word for word. This makes it easier to use in the program booklet or to publish on social media or a website. They will be grateful if they can adopt both without significant adjustments. They also depend on gripping texts to promote their events and fill the cinemas. The better a logline and synopsis are formulated, the more attractive the film will be for the festivals.

A logline and synopsis should ideally be in a plain text file that makes it as convenient as possible for third-party users to copy them. You also need to integrate them into the press kit of your film. But more about that later.

8

BIOGRAPHY & FILMOGRAPHY

I n the next step, you should prepare a presentable brief biography and filmography. Present yourself from your best side, informally and loosely. You are not applying to a bank. Again, keep it as short and concise as possible. And try to keep everything under 800 characters. That is not easy and can be a challenge. If you fail, write a more extended biography, and ask a friend to shorten it to less than 800 characters. Usually, outsiders have a better view of what is essential and what can be cut.

If you have won significant prizes, you should mention them. But please proceed carefully here. Awards from festivals which nobody knows anything about shouldn't appear in the biography. The same applies to festival participations. If your last film was shown at Sundance, it makes sense to mention that. However, if it was only shown at the 2nd New World Film Festival in wherever, omit it. At least, at this point. To include it seems highly unprofessional.

Here is an example of what a biography for the marketing of a short film could look like:

Pascal M. Meier was born in 1987 and raised in a small town close to the Black Forest in the south of Germany. From 2007 to 2010 he did Film and Video Training at ARRI Film & TV in Berlin, Germany. After that, he worked as an editor. From 2010 to 2017 he studied Directing at the Film Academy Vienna, under the Academy Award and two time Palme d'Or winner Michael Haneke. In 2015 and 2017 he went to Cannes as a participant of the Cannes Young Lions Competition. In 2018 he was a participant of the Berlinale Talent Campus. He went on to win several national and international awards for his work and his graduate film LET'S DO IT was not only shown at the Semaine de la Critique in Cannes, but also won a Student Academy Award. Currently, he is working on his first feature film.

The filmography generally accompanies the biography. In there you list as clearly as possible the films you have already shot. For example, in this format:

Year: Film title (Running Time, Genre, Country).

This could look like this, for example:

EXPERIENCE AS DIRECTOR (EXCERPT)

2016: #SELFIE *(7 Min, Comedy, Germany)*

2015: WE COULD HAVE, WE SHOULD HAVE, WE DIDN'T… *(13 Min, Drama, Germany)*

2013: IN FUTURE *(63 Min, Documentary, Russia)*

2012: SORRY TO INTERRUPT (*13 Min, Documentary, Germany*)

2011: IN THE NICK OF TIME (*12 Min, Dramedy, Germany*)

If you have already shot a long list of films, limit yourself to the most relevant five to ten projects and put the word "excerpt" behind the headline.

If you have won a significant award with one of your projects, you can also mention this in the filmography. But again, please only list truly world-renowned awards.

Like the logline and synopsis, the biography and filmography should be in a plain text file so that third party users can copy and paste them as easily as possible. The best file formats for this are TXT or WORD documents.

Biography and filmography are also integrated into the press kit.

9
_____

DIRECTOR'S PHOTO

F ilm festivals and other institutions will almost always
ask for a photo of the director. Here, experiments are
not so welcome; so you should have a profile photo at hand,
in which you are recognizable. Images where you hide
behind cameras, have your fingers in front of your face
Hitchcock style, or are otherwise difficult to spot are not
very popular.

The photo should preferably be a JPEG or TIF file with 300
dpi, which is smaller than 3 MB.

41

10

PRESS KIT

The EPK (Electronic Press Kit), a press kit in digital form, is very popular and useful in the short film sector. Therefore, I would also advise you to create one. It should summarize the most relevant information about your film as concisely as possible. If this is done in a visually appealing way, all the better.

As a rule, the press kit is a multi-page PDF document. Recently, many filmmakers have started using websites instead. But whether it is a website or a PDF, the content is always the same. In the best-case scenario, you have both.

After reviewing the press kit, the reader should have a clear picture of what your film is about, who shot it, where it has been shown so far, what awards it has won and what screening copies are available. The press kit is thus a central element for promoting your film, but also for summarizing crucial technical information.

Usually, the press kit contains the logline and synopsis, the director's biography, the filmography, the director's photo, at least one film still, a compressed cast and crew list, and the most important technical data. It often also includes a director's statement, the festival vita of the film, the film poster, and, if applicable, excerpts from press articles or jury discussions.

Recently, many press kits also contain links to the trailer or scenes from the film, as well as the film's website or social media pages. Sometimes they even include the viewing link.

In addition, the press kit should contain all the necessary contact information of the director, production, and distribution.

Press Kit Checklist

ESSENTIAL

- Title of the film / Original and English translation
- Logline and short synopsis
- Short bio and filmography of the director
- Director's photo
- Film stills
- Festival vita and awards
- Poster
- Compressed cast and crew list
- Technical specifications

OPTIONAL

- Link to trailer or clips from the film
- Director's commentary or interview with the director

- Biography and filmography of other cast-and-crew members
- Excerpts from press articles or other film reviews

I have already covered the logline, synopsis, biography, filmography, and director's photo. In the following, I will quickly discuss the other elements of the Press Kit.

11

TECHNICAL SPECIFICATIONS

To easily forward all the technical details of your film, it helps to collect them in one place. The press kit is perfect for this.

The technical specifications should, in any case, contain the following information:

• **Country of Production.** Where was the film produced? If more than one country is involved, list them according to their participation.

• **Year and Month of Production.** When was the film completed?

IMPORTANT! This should be the date when the film was shown for the first time, and in public. At this point, you should be extremely careful, because short films can usually only be screened at film festivals for about two years. An older film can't be submitted to most festivals. Festivals, television stations and video-on-demand services are more interested in newer productions. That is a pity, but unfortunately, it is the reality. Therefore: Don't make your film older than it is! Only when it has had its festival premiere does the clock start ticking. Only then was it put into the world. If your film hasn't had a premiere yet, here is where you enter the date when it is expected to have one, at the latest, or leave it completely open and write "looking for a premiere".

• **Genre / Category.** To which genre would your film most likely belong? And which relevant topics does it deal with? The most common genres for short films are drama, comedy, dramedy, horror, romance, genre film, etc. And the most common categories are Fiction, Documentary, Experimental, LGBT, Youth, Children, Human Rights, Travel, Nature, Ethno, Urbanism, Music-Video, etc. Your film can, of course, fall into several categories. Then you should list them according to their weighting.

• **Running Time.** I think this category is self-explanatory. To avoid confusion, you should list your film's running time in this format: hh:mm:ss.

• **Shooting Format.** Shooting format is the term used to describe how and in what resolution your film was shot. For example, digital, 4K. Or maybe 16 mm. You can also specify the camera that was used for the shooting - for example, RED Scarlet, 2K.

• **Animation Techniques**. If your film is an animation, you should describe here the methods you have used - for example, Drawing, Stop Motion, Motion Capture, Rotoscoping, etc.

• **Screening Copies.** What formats are available for screening? Ideally, you should have a DCP, a ProRes and an MP4 or MOV. If so, list them all in this order: DCP, ProRes 422, MP4 (1080p), Blu-ray, DVD.

• **Aspect Ratio.** What is the film's format? Possible formats are, for example: 1:1.37 / 1:1.66 / 1:1.85 / 1:2.35 / etc.

• **Sound.** Which sound format is available? Mono, Stereo, Dolby Digital, DTS, etc.?

• **Colour.** Is the film black and white or in colour? Or both?

• **Language.** What language is spoken? If several languages are spoken, list them according to their weighting in the film.

• **Subtitles.** Which subtitles are available? If the film's dialogues are not spoken in English, there should be at least English subtitles.

12

CAST AND CREW LIST

In the Press Kit you should list the production companies as well as the following team members with first and last names:

- Main Cast
- Producer
- Director
- Screenwriter
- Director of Photography
- Production Design
- Costume Designer
- Sound
- Editor
- Sound Design
- Music

It may happen that a festival or other institution will ask you to submit a cast and crew list. That's a list of all credits. And in the order and detail, they are mentioned in the opening and closing credits of the film. It is best to save this list as a PDF document in your movie folder.

13

DIRECTOR'S STATEMENT

I f you have the time and leisure to do so, you can include a short synopsis as well as a more extended summary and a director's statement or an interview with the director. This will set you apart from a large number of competitors.

I believe that the director's commentary is one of the most underestimated and least used ways to promote your film. Cleverly written, it can make a significant impact. It can tip the scales, so to speak, and make your film interesting for curators.

In the director's statement, you can explain your motivation and vision. Why was it vital for you to make this film? What inspired you to make it? What is your interpretation of the script? What is the actual theme of the film for you? What moves you?

You also have the opportunity to address the specifics of your project, things that might otherwise have escaped the viewer's attention. For example, you can tell how you managed to get the production going without a budget or how you managed to convince a famous actor to play the leading role. Even little anecdotes from the set are always a pleasure to read.

But here too, keep it short. The director's commentary should contain a maximum of 800 characters. It is still a short film.

To get the feel of a catchy director's statement, I recommend to you Darren Aronofsky's comment on his film, "mother!":

"It is a mad time to be alive. As the world population nears 8 billion we face issues too serious to fathom: ecosystems collapse as we witness extinction at an unprecedented rate; migrant crises disrupt governments; a seemingly schizophrenic US helps broker a landmark climate treaty and months later withdraws; ancient tribal disputes and beliefs continue to drive war and division; the largest iceberg ever recorded breaks off an Antarctic ice shelf and drifts out to sea. At the same time we face issues too ridiculous to comprehend: in South America, tourists twice kill rare baby dolphins that washed ashore, suffocating them in a frenzy of selfies; politics resembles sporting events; people still starve to death while others can order any meat they desire. As a species our footprint is perilously unsustainable yet we live in a state of denial about the outlook for our planet and our place on it. From this primordial soup of angst and helplessness, I woke up one morning and this movie poured out of me like a fever dream. All of my previous films gestated with me for many years but I wrote the first draft of mother! in 5 days. Within a year we were rolling cameras. And now two years later, it is an honor to return to the Lido for the world premiere. I imagine people may ask why the film has such a dark vision. Hubert Selby Jr., the author of Requiem for a Dream, taught me that through staring into the darkest parts of ourselves is where we find the light. mother! begins as a chamber story about a marriage. At the center is a woman who is asked to give and give and give until she can give nothing more. Eventually, the chamber story can't contain the pressure boiling inside. It becomes something else which is hard to explain or describe. I can't fully pinpoint where this film all came from. Some came from the headlines we face every second of every day, some came from the endless buzzing of notifications on our smartphones, some came from living through the blackout of Hurricane Sandy in downtown Manhattan, some came from my heart, some from my gut. Collectively it's a recipe I won't ever be able to reproduce, but I do know this serving is best drunk as a single dose in a shot glass. Knock it back. Salute!"[1]

What a great director's statement! After reading it, one has the urgent need to see this film, right?

Although it is about a feature film, it could just as well be about a short film.

* * *

WARNING: A director's commentary can also quickly have the opposite effect. For example, if you have made an experimental film full of metaphors but fail to write down your thoughts and motivations in an understandable way, the chance is high that it will backfire.

* * *

---

1. The Playlist, https://theplaylist.net/mother-directors-statement-20170829/

14

FESTIVAL VITA

I also highly recommend you include the festival vita of the film in the press kit. In other words, a list of when and where your masterpiece was shown and what prizes you could win.

From experience, I can say that there is a connection between the length of this list and the chances of being included in the program of other festivals.

Therefore, I would advise you to list every screening of your film in the press kit (and on the submission platforms). You should update this list regularly, especially on the platforms themselves.

The festival vita must contain the most important information about the respective screenings. It should indicate where and in what context the film was shown.

I would advise you to list the following information:

- **Name.** What is the name of the festival, event, or institution that will or has shown the film?

- **Edition.** For festivals, especially the established ones, of course, you should list which edition it is.
- **Program.** In which section was your film shown. Did it participate in a competition (int'l. competition) or a side program? If you want to make it easy for yourself, you can leave this category out.
- **Location.** In which city did the festival take place?
- **Country.** In which country did it take place?
- **Award.** If you were able to win an award at one of these events, you should clearly emphasize that.

I would then list the festivals in the following format:

dd.mm.yyyy * FESTIVAL NAME (Category/Program, City, Country) *AWARD*

This could look like this:

- 14.05.2020 * 73rd FESTIVAL DE CANNES *(Official Selection, 59th Semaine de la Critique, France)* ***RAIL D'OR AWARD***
- 26.05.2020 * 17th VIENNA INDEPENDENT SHORTS *(Opening Ceremony, Vienna, Austria)*
- 13.06.2020 * 48th HUESCA INTERNATIONAL FILM FESTIVAL *(Official Selection, Huesca, Spain)* ***ALBERTO SÁNCHEZ SPECIAL AWARD***
- 22.06.2020 * 16th FEST - NEW DIRECTORS | NEW FILMS FESTIVAL *(Official Selection, Espinho, Portugal)* ***BEST SHORT***
- 30.07.2020 * 69th MELBOURNE INT'L FILM FESTIVAL *(Out of Competition, Australia)*
- 21.09.2020 * 15th INT'L HUMAN RIGHTS FILM FESTIVAL ALBANIA *(Official Selection, Tirana, Albania)*
- …

15

TRAILER

Film trailers are also an excellent way of advertising. The main goal should be to attract attention and arouse interest in the film. The trailer should not reveal more than what is written in the logline. After all, you want to advertise the film and not spoil it.

In the short film sector, teasers are often used instead of trailers. These usually consist of only one shot from the film, combined with the insertion of the title.

If you decide to cut a trailer or teaser, keep it as short as possible. Don't forget that you are promoting a short film and not the latest Hollywood blockbuster. Therefore, it is better to avoid fade-ins like "A film by ..." or actors' crediting unless you have someone world-famous onboard.

Use the most spectacular shot or a captivating dialogue snippet, add a title, and the trailer/teaser is ready. Anything between a few seconds and half a minute is ideal for a trailer in the short film sector.

* * *

IMPORTANT! It does not always make sense to cut a trailer. For example, it is probably absurd to create a trailer if the movie has a running time of only one minute. Or to make a two-minute trailer for a five-minute short film. So it depends a little bit on the length of the movie if you need a trailer or not.

* * *

16

POSTER

B esides the logline, the poster is often the first thing a potential audience sees of your film. Make sure it is not the last.

A fancy film poster can open many doors for a film. Although it is not obligatory for submission to festival and many filmmakers, you could do without it; but I strongly advise you to make that effort.

You can find examples of successful film posters online en masse. Meanwhile, there are also many free or cheap templates that you can use as a starting point for your poster creation.

If your Photoshop skills aren't elaborate enough, you can find designers on freelance platforms (such as Fverr.com, Upwork.com, or 99designs.com) who will create great results for a small fee.

* * *

TIP: If you already have them, you should also include the laurels of film festivals that showed the film, as well as references to awards and praising lines from film reviews on your poster. But do not overdo it. If you print laurels from festivals which nobody knows on the poster, it makes a very unprofessional impression.

17

A FEW WORDS ABOUT THE FESTIVAL LAURELS

L aurels have been a symbol of outstanding achievements for thousands of years. In the past they were worn on the head; today they are printed on film posters. If you look at a depiction of Julius Caesar, his head will most likely be decorated by a laurel wreath. And if you look at the poster of the last great independent cinema hit, the chances are high that the branches and leaves of the laurel bush are printed on it somewhere. They usually frame the name of a prestigious festival where the film was awarded or screened.

Film festivals and filmmakers began to use laurels as a symbol of distinction sometime in the middle of the 20th century. Since then, they have frequently been used for advertising, both for the film and the festivals themselves.

Over time this method has become more and more established, and nowadays you can ask any festival that showed your film for the laurels, and they will send you a JPEG, TIFF, or PSD file. However, this does not mean that you should necessarily do that.

Posters pasted up with dozens of laurels from festivals that hardly anyone knows have not been generating admiration for some time. On the contrary, such use of laurels seems downright unprofessional.

But I don't want to advise against using laurels in general, because they can have a very positive influence on a film's career; you just shouldn't overdo it.

So place only the most significant laurels for your film on the poster, in the trailer, or at the beginning of the screening copies. If your film has only been shown at rather unknown festivals, it is better to do without the laurels altogether.

18

WEBSITE

I f curators, agencies, or viewers like a film, they usually research further information about the filmmakers. That's why nowadays, it is almost obligatory to create a website or at least a social media site for your film. Preferably both at once. But more about this in a later chapter.

19

A SAMPLE PRESS KIT

For any activity in the film distribution you need (here again, summarized) the following material:

ESSENTIAL

- 3-5 film stills
- logline
- synopsis
- director's photo
- biography and filmography of the director
- press kit

ADVANCED

- poster of the film
- director's statement
- subtitles in other languages
- cast and crew list
- trailer

- web page (or social media page)
- biography and filmography of other team members
- making of (photos and/or video)

Most of this information and materials should be collected in the press kit. That could look like this, for example:

SHORT FILM DISTRIBUTION

SYNOPSIS

A couple on holiday in Berlin. Everything is perfect, but then he wants to take a selfie...
The ending of a relationship as seen through a mobile phone.

** Pärchen-Urlaub in Berlin. Alles ist wunderbar, doch dann will er ein Selfie machen...
Das Ende einer Liebe, aus Handyperspektive.*

** Una pareja de vacaciones en Berlín. Todo parece perfecto pero él quiere tomarse una
selfie... El final de la relación vista a través de un teléfono celular.*

CURRICULUM VITAE

DAVID M. LORENZ

alive since 1985
telling stories since 1988
writing stories since 1991
drawing comics since 1993
directing movies since 1995
working for the movies since 2001

His fictional and documental short films were successfully
screened at more than 600 film festivals or events in over
60 countries worldwide / www.davidmlorenz.de

EXPERIENCE AS DIRECTOR (EXCERPT)

2016: #SELFIE (7 Min)
2015: WIR KÖNNTEN, WIR SOLLTEN, WIR HÄTTEN DOCH... / WE SHOULD HAVE, WE
COULD HAVE, WE DIDN'T... (13 Min)
2013: IN ZUKUNFT / IN FUTURE (63 Min)
2012: ENTSCHULDIGEN SIE BITTE DIE KURZE STÖRUNG / SORRY TO INTERRUPT (13 Min)
2011: EIN AUGENBLICK IN MIR / IN THE NICK OF TIME (12 Min)
2008: DES TEUFELS GRILLER ODER WIE ICH ZUM KÄSEKRAINER WURDE (15 Min)

CAST, CREW, FESTIVALS & CO.

#selfie

End of production:	11/2016
Country	Germany
Genre	Short, Dramedy
Director & Screenplay	David M. Lorenz
Production	FILMMENSCHEN GBR
	David M. Lorenz
	Paul Weiss
1st AD	Paul Weiss
Director of Photography	Martin Gasch
Sound	Inge Naning
Make Up	Sarah Huzel
Editor	David M. Lorenz
Music	The Turtles
Sound Design	Hans Morricone
Animation	Paul Weiss
Grading	Fabienne Bayer

Festivals (Official Selections & Awards):

14.11.2016 * 20th TALLINN BLACK NIGHTS FILM FESTIVAL - 17th SLEEPWALKERS INT'L SHORT FILM FESTIVAL *(Baltic Sea Competition, Estonia)*
BEST SHORT
14.11.2016 * 32nd INTERFILM – INT'L SHORT FILM FESTIVAL BERLIN *(Official Selection, Germany)*
03.12.2016 * 14th INT'L SHORT & INDEPENDENT FILM FESTIVAL *(Official Selection, Dhaka, Bangladesh)*
06.12.2016 * 14th BOGOSHORTS - BOGOTÁ SHORT FILM FESTIVAL *(Official Selection, Colombia)*
23.01.2017 * 27th BAMBERG SHORT FILM FESTIVAL *(Official Selection, Germany)*
14.02.2017 * 33rd INT'L FESTIVAL SARAJEVO "SARAJEVO WINTER" *(Official Selection, Bosnia and Herzegovina)*
17.02.2017 * 17th FILUMS - INT'L FILM FESTIVAL *(Official Selection, Lahore, Pakistan)*
10.03.2017 * 9th INTERNATIONALES MEDIENFESTIVAL *(Official Selection, Villingen-Schwenningen, Germany)*
BEST SHORT

SHORT FILM DISTRIBUTION

11.03.2017   * 21st VIDEONALE *(Official Selection, Berlin, Germany)*
SPECIAL MENTION
21.03.2017   * 10th CINÉGLOBE INTERNATIONAL FILM FESTIVAL AT CERN (Official Selection, Meyrin, Switzerland)
30.03.2017   * 10th TAOS SHORTZ FILM FESTIVAL *(Official Selection, New Mexico, USA)*
OOTO - OUT OF THE ORDINARY - HONORABLE MENTION
04.04.2017   * 29th FILMFEST DRESDEN *(Open Air Program, Germany)*
07.04.2017   * 7th NEW VISION INT'L SHORT FILM FESTIVAL *(Official Selection, Kiev, Ukraine)*
11.04.2017   * 6th LE COURTS NOUS TIENT *(Official Selection, Paris, France)*
13.04.2017   * 18th SCHWEINFURTER KURZFILMTAGE *(Official Selection, Germany)*
19.04.2017   * 12th ANNUAL MYRTLE BEACH FILM FESTIVAL *(Official Selection, South Carolina, USA)*
25.04.2017   * 18th CELLU L'ART SHORT FILM FESTIVAL JENA *(Official Selection, Germany)*
08.05.2017   * 15th INT'L SHORT FILM FESTIVAL - LA.MEKO *(Official Selection, Landau, Germany)*
10.05.2017   * 8th SKEPTO INTERNATIONAL FILM FESTIVAL *(Official Selection, Cagliari, Italy)*
13.05.2017   * 14th NEIßE FILM FESTIVAL *(Open Air Screening, Germany)*
17.05.2017   * 19th BACKUP_FESTIVAL *(backup.at.home Competition, Weimar, Germany)*
29.05.2017   * 7th INTERNATIONAL FILM FESTIVAL FICALJ *(Official Selection, Mérida, Venezuela)*
09.06.2017   * 24th RÜSSELSHEIMER KURZFILMTAGE *(Official Selection, Germany)*
13.06.2017   * 13th FESTIVAL DES NOUVEAUX CINÉMAS 2017 *(Official Selection, Paris, France)*
14.06.2017   * 10th PORTO7 - OPORTO INT'L FILM FESTIVAL *(Official Selection, Porto, Portugal)*
BEST INT'L FICTION FILM
20.06.2017   * 23rd PALM SPRINGS INT'L SHORTFEST AND FILM MARKET *(Film Market, Palm Springs, CA, USA)*
23.06.2017   * 8th FREDERICK FILM FESTIVAL *(Official Selection, Frederick, Maryland, USA)*
24.06.2017   * 15th ISCHIA FILM FESTIVAL *(Official Selection, Italy)*
BEST SHORT FILM
28.06.2017   * 18th CORTOGENIA SHORT FILM FESTIVAL *(Official Selection, Madrid, Spain)*
01.07.2017   * 18th SHORTS - INT'L FILM FESTIVAL *(Maremetraggio Section, Trieste, Italy)*
04.07.2017   * 3rd QUARANTINE FILM FESTIVAL 2017 *(Official Selection, Varna, Bulgaria)*
SPECIAL MENTION
11.07.2017   * 14th ÓBERA EN CORTOS - INT'L SHORT FILM FESTIVAL *(Official Selection, Oberá Misones, Argentina)*
12.07.2017   * 15th SHORTS AT MOONLIGHT *(Official Selection, Frankfurt, Germany)*
13.07.2017   * 14th INDY FILM FEST 2017 *(Official Selection, Indianapolis, Indiana, USA)*
14.07.2017   * 40th FESTIVAL INT'L INDEPENDIENTE *(Official Selection, Valencia, Spain)*
BEST EUROPEAN SHORT FILM
20.07.2017   * 8th KURZFILMNACHT AUGSBURGER LECHFLIMMERN *(Official Selection, Germany)*
26.07.2017   * 7th POSTIRA SEASIDE FILM FESTIVAL *("Midnight Shorts", Croatia)*
28.07.2017   * 11th FÜNF SEEN FILMFESTIVAL *(Short Film Competition "Goldene Glühwürmchen", Gilching, Germany)*
08.08.2017   * 15th MOLISE CINEMA FESTIVAL *(Official Selection, Casacalenda, Campobasso, Molise, Italy)*
10.08.2017   * 41st OPEN AIR FILMFEST WEITERSTADT *(Official Selection, Weiterstadt, Germany)*
21.08.2017   * 7th FARCUME - FESTIVAL INT'L DE CURTAS-METRAGENS DE FARO *(Official Selection, Faro, Algarve, Portugal)*
01.09.2017   * 10th CINEMA CITY INT'L FILM FESTIVAL *(Up to 10 000 bucks program, Novi Sad, Serbia)*
08.09.2017   * 14th JAMESON CINEFEST MISKOLC INT'L FILM FESTIVAL *(Official Selection, Hungary)*
11.09.2017   * 6th VISIONI CORTE INT'L SHORT FILM FESTIVAL *(Official Selection, Minturno, Italy)*
13.09.2017   * 15th AROUCA FILM FESTIVAL *(Official Selection, Portugal)*
20.09.2017   * 18th CALGARY INT'L FILM FESTIVAL *(Official Selection, Canada)*
23.09.2017   * 10th NAPERVILLE INDEPENDENT FILM FESTIVAL *(Official Selection, IL, USA)*
24.09.2017   * 6th INT'L SHORT FILM FESTIVAL VISION *(Official Selection, Voroshilova, Siberia, Russia)*
01.10.2017   * 1st JINZHEN INT'L FILM FESTIVAL IN HANCHENG *(Official Selection, China)*
05.10.2017   * 12th SAPPORO INT'L SHORT FILM FESTIVAL & MARKET *(Official Selection, Japan)*
05.10.2017   * 12th TACOMA FILM FESTIVAL *(Official Selection, Tacoma, Washington, USA)*
11.10.2017   * 10th LVIV INTERNATIONAL SHORT FILM FESTIVAL WIZ-ART *(Official Selection, Lviv, Ukraine)*
12.10.2017   * 6th FESTIVAL DE COURTS MÉTRAGES DE LA COTE BLEUE *(Official Selection, Carry l Rouet, Provence, France)*

DAVID M. LORENZ

12.10.2017 * 15th TALLGRASS FILM FESTIVAL *(Official Selection, Wichita, KS, USA)*
14.10.2017 * 7th INT'L SHORT FILM FESTIVAL OF CYPRUS *(Official Selection, Cyprus)*
18.10.2017 * 15th SHNIT WORLDWIDE SHORTFILMFESTIVAL *(Official Selection, Bern, Switzerland)*
21.10.2017 * 3rd FÜRSTENWALDER FILMTAGE PARKFLIMMERN *(Official Selection, Berlin, Germany)*
23.10.2017 * 16th MUESTRA INT'L DE CORTOMETRAJES "JUJUY / CORTOS" *(Official Selection, Argentina)*
28.10.2017 * 36th FESTIVAL DU CINÉMA INT'L EN ABITIBI-TÉMISCAMINQUE *(Official Selection, Canada)*
31.10.2017 * 15th CATACUMBA UNDERGROUND FILM FESTIVAL *(Official Selection, Godella, Valencia, Spain)*
01.11.2017 * 9th JANA INT'L FILM FESTIVAL FOR CHILDREN & YOUTH *(Official Selection, Lebanon)*
03.11.2017 * 7th FESTIVAL INT'L DE CINE EDUCATIVO Y ESPIRITUAL CIDUAD RODRIGO *(Official Selection, Spain)*
05.11.2017 * 6th CINEPHONE - INT'L SMARTPHONE FILM FESTIVAL *(Official Selection, Barcelona, Spain)*
08.11.2017 * 25th ALTER-NATIVE INT'L SHORT FILM FESTIVAL *(Official Selection, Tirgu Mures, Romania)*
09.11.2017 * 5th WAG FILM FESTIVAL *(Official Selection, Terranuova Bracciolini, Italy)*
10.11.2017 * 8th INT'L MOBILE FILM FESTIVAL *(Official Selection, Bitola, Macedonia)*
11.11.2017 * 19th INT'L SHORT FILM FESTIVAL OF THE BAY OF PASAIA - IKUSKA *(Official Selection, Trintxerpe, Spain)*
11.11.2017 * 11th ANNUAL RED ROCK FILM FESTIVAL *(Official Selection, Cedar City, Utah, USA)*
15.11.2017 * 17th FLENSBURGER KURZFILMTAGE *(Official Selection, Germany)*
16.11.2017 * 22nd ERRENTERIA SHORT FILM FESTIVAL *(Official Selection, Errenteria, Guipúzcoa, Spain)*
            BEST SHORT
20.11.2017 * 14th KINOFILM - MANCHESTER INT'L SHORT FILM & ANIMATION FESTIVAL *(Official Selection, U.K.)*
27.11.2017 * 31st SCHWENNINGER KURZFILMFESTIVAL *(Official Selection, Germany)*
27.11.2017 * 35th FESTIVAL TOUS COURTS *(Youth Program, Aix en Provence, France)*
01.12.2017 * 13th FESTIVAL DE CINE Y VINO *(Official Selection, La Solana, Spain)*
01.12.2017 * 9th PILAS EN CORTO - FESTIVAL INT'L DE CORTOMETRAJES *(Official Selection, Spain)*
06.12.2017 * 22nd LINEA D'OMBRA FESTIVAL *(Official Selection, Salerno, Italy)*
21.01.2018 * 5th SUDAN INDEPENDENT FILM FESTIVAL (SIFF) 2018 *(Official Selection, Khartoum, Sudan)*
28.01.2018 * 6th LA MIDA NO IMPORTA - INT'L FILM FESTIVAL *(Official Selection, Barcelona, Spain)*
30.01.2018 * 2nd INDIEJUNIOR ALLIANZ - INT'L CHILDREN'S AND YOUTH FILM FESTIVAL *(Official Selection, Porto, Portugal)*
05.02.2018 * 7th FESTIVAL INT'L DE CINE DE PEHUAJO *(Official Selection, Argentina)*
11.02.2018 * 18th BRUSSELS INDEPENDENT FILM FESTIVAL *(Official Selection, Brussels, Belgium)*
15.03.2018 * 13th ATHENS ANIMFEST *(Official Selection, Athens, Greece)*
05.04.2018 * 5th SHORTY WEEK FILM FEST *(Official Selection, Cádiz, Spain)*
18.04.2018 * 18th INDEPENDENT DAYS INTERNATIONAL FILM FESTIVAL 2018 *(Official Selection, Karlsruhe, Germany)*
21.04.2018 * 5th CENSURADOS FILM FESTIVAL *(Official Selection, Lima, Peru)*
23.04.2018 * 4th SYDNEY WORLD FILM FESTIVAL *(Official Selection, Sydney, Australia)*
27.04.2018 * 6th FRONT RANGE FILM FESTIVAL *(Official Selection, Longmont, CO, USA)*
05.05.2018 * 10th FILM FEST PETALUMA *(Official Selection, Petaluma, CA, USA)*
21.05.2018 * 15th MOSTRA CINEMA TARANTO *(Official Selection, Taranto, Italy)*
24.05.2018 * 10th ROLLE VORWÄRTS - FLENSBURGER KURZFILMTAGE *(Official Selection, Germany)*
31.05.2018 * 13th BERKSHIRE INTERNATIONAL FILM FESTIVAL *(Official Selection, Great Barrington, MA, USA)*
18.06.2018 * 10th ZEITIMPULS KURZFILMWETTBEWERB *(Official Selection, Vienna, Austria)*
30.06.2018 * 19th SHORTS - INT'L SHORT FILM FESTIVAL *(Best of Shorts IFF, Trieste, Italy)*
01.08.2018 * 10th MALTA SHORT FILM FESTIVAL *(Official Selection, Malta)*
            MOST ORIGINAL CONCEPT & *BEST EDITING* & *FOREIGN JURY AWARD*
25.08.2018 * 18th BLISSFEST333 INTERNATIONAL FILM FESTIVAL *(Official Selection, Denver, CO, USA)*
25.08.2018 * 21st CALIFORNIA INDEPENDENT FILM FESTIVAL *(Sapporo Short Fest Special Screening, Orinda, USA)*

20.09.2018   * 4th FILMFEST BREMEN *(Official Selection, Bremen, Germany)*
BEST INNOVATION AWARD
04.10.2018   * 8th FESTIVAL INTERNACIONAL DE CINE FINE ARTS *(Official Selection, Miramar, Puerto Rico)*
08.10.2018   * 5th FESTIVAL MUNDIAL DE CINE EXTREMO - WORLD FILM FESTIVAL OF VERACRUZ *(Official Selection, Veracruz, Mexico)*
12.10.2018   * 14th INDIGO FILMFEST *(Official Selection, Wadern-Bardenbach, Germany)*
13.10.2018   * 7th BRISTOL RADICAL FILM FESTIVAL *(Official Selection, Bristol, UK)*
02.11.2018   * 5th BUFFALO DREAMS FANTASTIC FILM FESTIVAL *(Official Selection, Buffalo, NY, USA)*
DREAMER AWARD FOR OUTSTANDING SHORT
14.11.2018   * 18th SHORT FILM DAYS FLENSBURG *(Best of Section, Germany)*
14.02.2019   * 4th INTERNATIONAL FILM FESTIVAL OF THE CARIBBEAN SEA *(Official Selection, Nueva Esparta, Venezuela)*
23.03.2019   * 23rd CINE-MANIACS FILMFEST *(Official Selection, Türkheim, Germany)*
13.04.2019   * HARZMOVIENALE 2019 *(Official Selection, Quedlinburg, Germany)*
JURY AWARD
08.05.2019   * 12th CORTI A PONTE - INT'L FILM FESTIVAL *(Official Selection, Padova, Italy)*
02.11.2019   * 22nd FESTIVAL INT'L DU COURT MÉTRAGE D' AIGUES-MORTES ‚ECRAN LIBRE' *(Official Selection, France)*
08.11.2019   * 23rd FESTIVAL ECRAN LIBRE *(Official Selection, Aigues-Mortes, France)*

"Showing creativity and resourcefulness in format, this short film is effective, timeless and timely in its comment on and portrayal of the consequences of modern society, also working well as a clever campaign against gender violence. All that glitters is not gold..."

JURY - 17th SLEEPWALKERS INT'L FILM FESTIVAL

"We humbly award this film with the Best Short Film Award for its precise use of modern technologies, for its intelligent use of parallel montage as well as for its clear and straight forward use of the cinematic discourse in such a limited time. With a final twist!"

JURY - 15th ISCHIA FILM FESTIVAL

"Der Trend der überhöhten Selbstdarstellung durch soziale Medien wird mit seinen eigenen Stilmitteln professionell und herausragend dargestellt. Eine gekonnte Kameraführung durch eine veränderte und ungewöhnliche Sichtweise, die des Selfies aus der Handyperspektive, ermöglicht dem Publikum einen anderen Blickwinkel. Dadurch wird ein gesellschaftlich relevantes Thema, die oft fehlende Sensibilität für unser unmittelbares Umfeld, mit einer Leichtigkeit und trotzdem tiefgehend emotional kommuniziert."

JURY - 9th MEDIENFESTIVAL

TECHNICAL SPECIFICATIONS

Location/s	Berlin, Germany
Running Time	07:00
Shooting Format	2K
	2
Shooting Days	
Screening Format	DCP, ProRes 422, MOV, MP4, BluRay, DVD
Aspect Ratio	16:9
Sound	Stereo
Language	English
Subtitles	English / German / French / Spanish / Italian / Chinese / Russian

CONTACTS

DISTRIBUTION
Name des
Verleihs
Riemannstr. 21
10961 Berlin
Germany
+49 (0) 176 - 54664299

film@namedesverleihs.de
www.namedesverleihs.de

PRODUCTION COMPANY
Name der Filmproduktion
Herr Mustermann

Skalitzer
Str.109
10997 Berlin
Germany
+49 (0) 177 5546354

mustermann@namederfilmproduktion.de
www.filmmenschen.de

DIRECTOR
David M.
Lorenz,
+49 (0) 176 843437192

kontakt@davidmlorenz.com
www.davidmlorenz.de

I used this press kit relatively successfully for my short film #selfie. If you want to use this version as a DOC template, please send me a short e-mail (contact@davidmlorenz.com), and I will send it to you.

20

WHAT IS THE GOAL?

The philosopher Seneca once wrote: "Let all your efforts be directed toward something, let them keep that goal in mind." This wise sentence was rediscovered and made a principle by Stephen Covey in his recommendable classic "The 7 Ways to Effectiveness".[1]

The principle is based on the idea that all things are created twice. First, there is a mental creation, i.e. an image of the desired result, which exists exclusively in your head. And later there is the physical creation, which can also be perceived by others.

I think it's worth listening to these two wise Stoics and to start the film distribution with a picture in mind, because it will be a long and sometimes arduous journey. A race, at times. Or even a marathon. And before you start running, you should - whatever metaphor you prefer - have a clear idea of where you are heading. Because if you don't have a goal in mind, the chances are high that you'll get lost somewhere in the rapidly growing world of festivals, online platforms, film agencies, and TV stations.

The more precise your objectives are at the beginning, the higher the chance of success. Sure, there will be (and should be) surprises along the way, and you may have to take one or two detours. But especially then it is vital to have a goal in mind that you can orient yourself by. So, it's best to take a few minutes now and think about precisely where you want to go. Sure, you are looking for an audience for your film. But try to be a little more precise.

What do you ideally want to achieve within the distribution? What degree of success do you wish for the film? How can you tell that you have reached your goal? What was the reason for making this film?

Maybe you'll brainstorm briefly on these questions or draw a quick mind map. The more detailed you get, the better.

Is the film distribution a success if you made it into a film festival and the first viewer laughs? Or do fifty festivals have to be in your film vita before you are satisfied? Maybe you don't care about film festivals and prefer to build a relationship with television stations? Or perhaps you are happy if you have your film placed in the program of a VoD provider. Or maybe you want to reach an even larger mass of people online, via free streaming providers? How many, actually?

To help your imagination a little bit, I have summarized the classic goals that filmmakers have in distributing their short films:

• **Receive a wide range of feedback.** If this is one of your first film projects, it might be exciting for you to get extensive (and preferably immediate) feedback on your work. You could get this, for example, at film festivals, through Q&A sessions, by talking to the audience, and through comments you receive after a release on online platforms and social networks. In any case, your priority would be to reach as many people as possible and provoke reactions.

• **Spread a message.** You made your film because a specific topic was close to your heart or because you wanted to share a strong message with the world. In this case, your primary concern will probably be to reach as many people as possible. But maybe you also want to reach a particular group of people. Then the question would be where to find them and the best way to address them.

• **Finding future comrades-in-arms and sponsors.** Maybe your primary goal is to promote yourself as a filmmaker. For example, you can use your film to find staff or sponsors for further projects. True to the motto "After the film is before the film", your work should serve as a business card. Maybe you already have your next project in the drawer, and you are only missing a few team members or the last building blocks in the financing. For this, more renowned film festivals and especially their associated film markets provide excellent opportunities to find like-minded people and future comrades-in-arms.

• **Travel the world.** There are a lot of film festivals out there. Most of the organizers are very interested in filmmakers presenting their works on location. It often happens that they invite not only a film but also the artists behind it. Directors and actors in particular are incredibly welcome festival guests.

Most festivals entice with a few overnight stays and accreditation for all events. This often includes interesting panels and workshops. Sometimes delicious food and drinks are available for free. Some festivals even cover travel expenses. And almost always great parties are thrown. So, film festivals offer an ideal opportunity to travel the world, discover other cultures, and meet people you wouldn't have met at home.

If travelling is one of your priorities, then the focus is clearly on getting as many festivals as possible excited about your film. And not just to wait for the big names to commit to your film. Maybe you also have specific countries in focus that you would like to visit.

• **Refinancing the film.** Despite all technical modernizations, film projects are often still expensive pleasures. Especially in the short film sector, much is paid out of one's pocket. This can quickly tear big holes in the budget. Maybe that's why it's your primary goal to plug them again. In other words: you want to recoup your production costs.

In this case, the first thing you should do is keep an eye on the prize money that the festivals offer. In addition to the big film festivals, which almost all offer quite generous sums of money, there are also quite a few smaller ones which also provide higher sums, but where the competition is much less fierce. Also, film festivals that pay a screening fee or sales of the film would bring you closer to this goal, which would argue in favour of advertising at renowned film markets.

• **Building an audience or fanbase.** If you succeed in building up a fanbase, you will have some advantages in the future. By fans I don't mean as many Facebook followers as possible, but rather an audience that is interested in your artistic development and your films. Firstly, it is simply incredibly motivating to know that there are people out there who follow what you do. And on the other hand, a large fanbase can help you with the most painful parts of the film process - financing and distribution - directly, for example through crowdfunding platforms or indirectly, with advice, ideas, contacts, etc.

If your goal is to have a loyal community around you, then it would be a good idea to invest a lot of time in the platform where you want to turn the audience into fans. For example, this could be your website, where you offer a newsletter and collect e-mail addresses or a Vimeo channel where you compete for followers.

• **Win a specific film award.** Of course, it is also possible that you aim to win a special film award. While this would not necessarily be a particularly helpful and desirable motive in the distribution (and the filmmaking process itself), it is undoubtedly a driving force for some filmmakers. So, if you want to win an Oscar for Best Short Film or the European Film Award, you should preferably submit your film to the festivals where you could qualify for submitting to exactly these film awards.

As you can see, you could pursue many goals in distributing your film, Just as there are numerous reasons to make a film. What were yours again? It's best to write down now what you want to achieve with your film in the coming months and why.

* * *

TIP: Of course, it is possible that you have several goals. But only up to a certain degree. At some point, there comes the time when you must decide to get married. If you have shouted "Here!" with all the goals described, then think about how much weight you give them. This will make many decisions in the future easier for you.

* * *

21

WHAT IS THE BUDGET?

One thing is for sure: Any film distribution will cost money and time. Even though it is often possible to recoup the financial investment, there are expenses to be made first. These can quickly add up to tidy amounts. Besides, appropriate distribution can be very time-consuming. But another thing is sure too: The more time and money you invest, the more successful your film will ultimately be. I have experienced this a thousand times in my professional career. In the end, the time and effort invested in film distribution will be reflected in the film's success in terms of its visibility.

But one thing is certain: you will not be able to exhaust all the possibilities of film distribution, neither in terms of time nor money. Even the biggest budget will reach its limits somewhere. That's why it's important that you not only think about the goal of the distribution, but also about your available budget and time. How much can you spend on film distribution? And how much time can you invest?

* * *

TIP: If your budget is tiny, this is no reason to be discouraged. It often happens that you can increase this budget by winning an award or selling your film. Besides, there are many festivals to which you can submit your film at a very low cost or even free of charge.

* * *

PART II

DISTRIBUTION

And there I was, in the middle of China. The vast sports stadium filled with hundreds of locals, and the music was loud - a smell of popcorn and stinky tofu was in the air. We were held behind a barrier tape and waited for further instructions. What would happen next? Somehow nobody had an answer to that.

Then the music got louder, and our names were blaring through the stadium speakers. The crowd cheered enthusiastically, and we followed the long blue carpet to our front row seats. We more or less shyly waved to the right and left while some Hans Zimmer evergreens were booming from the stadium speakers.

What a welcome for short filmmakers! The festival organizers entered the stage and officially opened the first short film festival in Hancheng. This was followed by the obligatory fireworks display for major Chinese events of this kind. We were suddenly rock stars.

While an orchestra began interpreting film classics of the last century, I relaxed and sank back into my seat to let this further stop on my short film's exciting journey take its full effect on me.

While listening to Ennio Morricone's songs, I indulged in memories of all the places to which my short film had led me. The breathtakingly beautiful old movie theatre in Recife came to my mind, as did the long and warm movie nights in Bogotá. I remembered seeing this short film in the snow on the marketplace in front of the Frauenkirche in Dresden and watching it on the beach in Varna, eating mussels and sipping white wine. People appeared before my inner eye. All the filmmakers, curators, organizers, or viewers with whom I am now friends, but also the fleeting acquaintances that have become ingrained.

Looking back, I am amazed where this little seven-minute short film, which my friends and I shot in Berlin within two days on a budget of only a few euros, took me. What a remarkable audience our work from back then could reach in the meantime. And finally, how much we got back for the energy and money we put into it!

There I was, sitting in this small village in China, and was very grateful. I looked around and had the feeling that it was not just me. All the filmmakers around me were similarly euphoric. Our films were selected from thousands of others that were shot this year. The festival had taken special care to ensure that only the most successful filmmakers of the past year were invited - the filmmakers whose works had made it into the programs of major festivals worldwide. However, what we had in common was - as it would later turn out - certainly not the fact that we had made the best films of the year. There were better ones. It was rather the fact that we had done some things right in the *distribution*.

22

THE BEST DISTRIBUTION STRATEGY

O n the surface, there seem to be many different approaches to short film distribution. But when you take a closer look at the subject matter, it quickly becomes apparent that there is a kind of recipe or strategy that almost all successful filmmakers and short film agencies follow ... and with good reason.

I will tell you this recipe, but it is only a basic one. Depending on your specific goals, you might want to adjust the details here and there. I will give you suggestions in the appropriate places and hope to answer all open questions about the best distribution strategy in the following chapters.

A short overview at the beginning. The basic ingredients in successful short film distribution are:

- An international premiere at a renowned festival.
- Festival screenings around the world.
- Sales to television stations and VoD services.
- Publication on other online platforms.

All professional short film distributions follow this master plan. There are only minor differences in the weighting of individual steps and in deciding when to take which steps, and to what extent they should or can overlap. So when it comes to such questions as how long should I send my film exclusively to festivals before I sell it to television stations? How long should I try to sell my film before I make it freely available on Vimeo? Does it make sense to do everything at once?

I will go into the individual steps in the following pages, and I think that if you read carefully, you will be able to answer these questions for yourself and your film afterwards.

23

THE INTERNATIONAL PREMIERE

The optimal short film career starts with a sensational premiere at a well-known international film festival. The more known the festival is, the better. Such a start for the film only brings advantages and is, therefore, part of every distribution strategy.

My advice to you is to take your time, especially at the beginning of film distribution. First, only submit to larger, well-known festivals and wait for the first confirmation.

This strategy has the following advantages:

• **Higher chances.** The larger festivals, in particular, continue to attach great importance to the fact that a film premieres at them. Even if it is not always explicitly requested, they prefer films that have never been shown anywhere before the festival begins. A few festivals can even still afford to accept only international or national premieres for submission. You simply have a higher (or the only) chance at these festivals if your film has not been shown elsewhere before. Take advantage of it.

• **Great Attention.** A world premiere at a renowned film festival can generate a lot of attention for your film and you. So if your film makes it to one of the most famous festivals in the world, it will be seen with different eyes; both by future viewers and by festival curators and buyers. In other words, the interest in your film will increase. For example, when it premieres in Clermont-Ferrand, I can guarantee that you will be offered many free festival submissions. And one or the other curators present will even include the film directly in the program without you having to submit it again. Smaller festivals, especially, like to adorn themselves with films that have debuted shown at the more renowned festivals. That attracts an audience.

In addition, larger festivals are usually associated with a film market. Curators and buyers from television stations or online channels and representatives of film agencies cavort there. These markets offer optimal opportunities for submission to other festivals, for finding agents, or for sales. For example, receiving an offer from a television station at one of these festivals could happen quickly. Or you may be approached by a distributor. All these attentions and possibilities are extremely helpful, especially at the beginning of the distribution, to get the film's career rolling.

But how do you manage to place your film in the program of one of these festivals? We will now come to that.

24

HOW FILM FESTIVALS WORK (AND WHY THEY ARE SO IMPORTANT)

There are many film festivals out there. Almost every city has its own nowadays, and new ones are born every day. Los Angeles alone offers over a hundred festivals a year--and that is a good thing. They are especially important for the short film because unlike feature films, this film niche has far fewer distribution opportunities.

Most film festivals take place once a year and show, over several days or even weeks, a selected program of films. Some festivals are more interested in films that appeal to a wide audience, and others prefer more experimental, less accessible cinema. Some festivals focus on a specific type of films, such as animation festivals and documentary film festivals. Some have very limited thematic focuses, such as sports film festivals, while others try to reflect international filmmaking as broadly as possible. Furthermore, each festival has its taste. This depends strongly on the respective curators as well as the audience and can, of course, change over the years.

It has become relatively easy to submit to festivals - for

example, online via various submission platforms. Then you pay a small fee (between 1.00 Euro and 3.00 Euro) to the portal and the festival. The latter can be more expensive, but there are also many festivals, especially in Europe, that do not charge this fee.

However, film festivals receive far more film submissions than they could accommodate in their program. Especially today, when it has become so much easier to make and send films, curators are drowning in submissions, especially around the festival deadlines.

As a result, there are several rounds of viewing, and often the organizers have to make difficult decisions for or against a film. This often leads to long and sometimes heated discussions between the curators.

Despite this flood of films, however, most film festivals attach great importance to the fact that they judge all film-makers and their films fairly. My own experience can only contradict rumours that films were rejected without ever having been seen. Even big festivals like Slamdance attach importance to at least two programmers seeing and evaluating a film.

Sure, it can happen that curators don't finish watching your film. But then that probably has more to do with the film itself. Most festival organizers have a well-trained eye and can quickly assess whether a film is suitable for their program or not. However, they are very keen to give every film the same chances.

So don't worry, festival curators are not some mysterious, alien species just waiting to align themselves against you. On the contrary, they are often great film enthusiasts or film-makers themselves, working voluntarily and with great passion for a good cause. All the curators I have met so far have always been sincere in their search for what they consider the best films of the season. And over the years I have been able to get to know quite a few of them.

Of course, your film should inspire at least one of these curators. One person from the committee has to *love* it. Otherwise, it will probably not make it into the program, unless you have some important names in the credits or already have a relationship with the festival, which showed previous works of yours.

I can guarantee you that, with a little patience and perseverance, you will find a film festival that chooses to show your film. To ensure that this search does not take too long, I will give you some advice on the best way to proceed.

25

WHICH FILM FESTIVALS ARE SUITABLE FOR THE INTERNATIONAL PREMIERE?

You have probably already asked yourself which festival is suitable as a premiere for your film. Now, that depends on various aspects:

• **The film.** First, the genre of your film will dictate which festivals are eligible for a premiere. For example, it doesn't make much sense to send a trashy horror film to Cannes or submit your experiment to Sundance. You can save those entry fees, which are not exactly low in either case.

If you have to be a bit careful about your finances, I advise you to do quick research before any expensive submission. It is effortless and not very time-consuming to find out what kind of film interests the festivals. Brief online research is sufficient. On the festivals' websites, you can often find the programs of the last editions. The descriptions of the films in them will help you quickly develop a feeling for the curators' preferences and focus. With a little effort, you will surely find one or the other of the program's films online.

* * *

TIP: A great help in getting started is to search for short films from past years that are similar to yours in form or content. If you come across such a film, you can research where it showed and submit it to the same or similar festivals. Nowadays, you can find out this information with just a few clicks.

* * *

FURTHERMORE, the premiere festival and the submission strategy itself will of course depend on the quality of your film. You should therefore ask yourself as early as possible whether it is strong enough to make it into the program of an A or B festival. This is where a fair amount of honesty with yourself is required. I know, it can be very sobering to have to admit that your film lacks that certain something. Or it's just not technically professional enough to make it into the short film Olympus. But it's even *more* frustrating *after* you've blown a lot of submission fees.

So it's best to gather as much feedback as possible right from the start, ideally from viewers who know the short film market well.

* * *

ATTENTION: You should not underestimate the potential of your film. Many inexperienced filmmakers tend to make their performance smaller than it is. Just because you do a little research on the festivals doesn't mean that you shouldn't experiment. On the contrary, especially at the beginning of the festival distribution, you have to be a risk-taker and courageous. In other words, you should also submit to some festivals where you think your chances are rather slim. I have experienced so many surprises in my film distribution work that I have come to the following conclusion: It's better to submit once more than once too few. Like every other aspect of the film business, festival distribution is always a balancing act between megalomania and modesty.

So once again, because it is so important: I generally advise you to take some risks in your submissions. In other words, send your film to festivals where you don't think you stand a chance. However, you should only do this up to a specific pain threshold, which you should determine in advance.

OF COURSE, it is also possible that you have made a high-quality film, but due to its theme, it is hardly suitable for a larger festival audience. Maybe you have produced a documentary about the last shepherds in the Carpathians or a very idiosyncratic, experimental film. You would then be well advised to submit your film to so-called niche festivals and festivals with a particular focus.

The larger niches here are documentaries, animated films, experimental films, and genre films. Moreover, the number of festivals that also cover smaller niches is growing rapidly. For instance, there are film festivals that show exclusively dance films. Others show films about mountain climbing. Still others focus on films shot on a cell phone, or films about moustaches (*International Moustache Film Festival*).

There is a festival somewhere for even the most bizarre and absurd films. In the truest sense of the word, the *Incredibly Strange Films Festival* in New Zealand is dedicated to the strangest films of the past year. Also at the popular *Interfilm Short Film Festival* in Berlin, Die lange Nacht des abwegigen

Films is undoubtedly one of the most popular happenings. Only films that were too different to be included in the other programs and the competition are shown there.

But back to the international premiere. Even among the niche festivals, a few have a certain reputation worldwide and could make a sensational premiere for your film. One example would be the *Sitges Festival Int'l de Cinema Fantàstic* de Catalunya, which is considered the world's most important event for fantastic film and is dedicated exclusively to this genre. Or the *Dok Leipzig*, one of the oldest film festivals globally, which shows documentary films without exception and enjoys an excellent reputation.

• **Your goals.** The choice of the premiere festival and the festival distribution, of course, depends on your intentions.

What do you want to achieve in the distribution? If your biggest goal is to sell the film as soon as possible, then a festival with a large market is probably the best choice. That could be the *Clermont-Ferrand Film Festival*, for example. The entire short film industry meets here. But if the primary goal is to generate a lot of publicity, then festivals that are known outside the short film scene, such as Sundance, are more suitable. Maybe you want to get as much feedback as possible first? Then you should look for festivals that have a large audience and where the respective short films are screened several times. Are awards and prize money the most important thing for you? Your chances will increase if you submit to smaller festivals with less competition.

• **The budget.** In the end, the choice of the premiere festival and the festival distribution depends on your budget. For example, almost all festival submissions are subject to fees. These can be very high, especially for American festivals. Therefore, your budget will most likely force you to make a particular choice. And you will probably have to miss out on one or the other submission.

Nonetheless, don't be put off too quickly by the sometimes very high entry fees. There are a few possibilities to reduce or even avoid these fees. But more about that later.

OKAY, those were the most critical factors on which your film premiere depends. But you're probably still sitting in front of a large number of film festivals, wondering where to start - i.e., which festivals you should take a closer look at.

Of course, I can't give you a complete answer to this question because I haven't seen your movie, but a few more hints and tips should help you.

One can say that there are a few so-called A-festivals that show short films. These are the film festivals that everybody knows, even people who have nothing or very little to do with film. Those would be the big festivals in Cannes, Utah (Sundance), Venice, Locarno, Toronto, Berlin, and maybe Tribeca.

The transition to the next league of film festivals is fluid and I am now walking on very thin ice. For our purposes, right up front is the biggest short film festival in the world in Clermont-Ferrand, and the festivals in Edinburgh, London (Raindance), Palm Springs, Busan, Atlanta, Austin (South by Southwest), Aspen, etc.

After all, there are many renowned film festivals to be considered for a sensational short film premiere. In the following, I have taken the trouble to list most of these more known festivals.

26

LIST OF PREMIERE FESTIVALS

I n the following, I have listed the festivals that are very well suited for an international film premiere for various reasons. Since it is in many ways hopeless to rank or prioritize them here, I have sorted them by the month of the event. Please note that the deadlines for submission are set much earlier.

While creating the overview, I have oriented myself on different lists that might be interesting to you:

• **List of Oscar-qualifying film festivals.** This list is published and maintained by the Academy of Motion Picture Arts and Sciences. If your film wins a top prize at one of the festivals listed here, you are qualified to submit your film to the Oscars. It is not easy to be included in this list, and the listed festivals have a certain reputation in the short film sector. You can retrieve this list here: https://www.oscars.org/sites/oscars/files/92aa_rule19_short_festivals.pdf

• **List of film festivals qualifying for the European Film Awards.** To submit to the European Film Awards, one must first be eligible. Here it is sufficient if the short film makes it into the competition of one of the festivals listed by the European Film Academy. It is not necessary to win a prize there. However, the list is much shorter: https://www.europeanfilmacademy.org/Links.38.0.html

• **Festival calendar of the *AG Kurzfilm*.** The AG Kurzfilm e. V. / Bundesverband Deutscher Kurzfilm (German Short Film Association) is doing a great job of making the short film itself and German short film, in particular, more popular. In addition to many interesting articles and statistics, they also publish an annual festival calendar, which contains an exquisite selection of mainly European film festivals. You can find this calendar here: https://ag-kurzfilm.de/de/festivalkalender.html

• **List of the *British Academy of Film and Television Arts (BAFTA)*.** The British Academy of Film and Television Arts has also published a list of festivals that qualify for the BAFTA Award. In this case, participation in the competition of one of the festivals listed here is sufficient: https://awards.bafta.org/sites/default/files/images/shorts_qualifying_festivals_list_2019_20.pdf

• **My own experiences.** Over the years, I have formed my opinion of short film festivals worldwide, and the following list contains my views.

I think that all the festivals on this list could offer an exciting premiere for your short film. The film festival you ultimately choose depends heavily on your goals and budget, however.

Short Film Festivals:

January

- Flickerfest ISFF, Sydney, Australia

February

- Clermont-Ferrand ISFF, France

March

- Regard - Saguenay ISFF, Canada
- Tampere ISFF, Finland

April

- Aspen Shortsfest, Colorado, USA
- Brussels SFF, Belgium
- Busan ISFF, South Korea
- Go Short ISFF, Nijmegen, Holland

May

- Krakow FF, Poland
- Oberhausen ISFF, Germany
- VIS – Vienna Shorts, Austria

June

- Hamburg ISFF, Germany
- Huesca IFF, Spain
- Norwegian SFF, Grimstad, Norway
- Palm Springs ISFF, CA, USA
- Los Angeles ISFF, CA, USA

July

- Curtas Vila do Conde IFF, Portugal
- DokuFest I Documentary and SFF, Prizren, Kosovo
- LA Shorts IFF, Los Angeles, CA, USA

August

- Holly Shorts FF, Los Angeles, CA, USA
- Odense IFF, Denmark
- Turku AFF, Turku, Finland

September

- 2ANNAS - Riga ISFF, Riga, Latvia
- DC Shorts, Washington DC, USA
- Drama SFF, Greece
- Encounters FF, Bristol, UK
- ISFF Lille, France
- Short Shorts FF & Asia, Tokyo, Japan

October

- Ghent SFF, Belgium
- Sao Paulo ISFF, Brazil
- Show Me Shorts FF, Auckland, New Zealand
- Uppsala ISFF, Sweden
- Valladolid SFF, Spain

November

- Alcine, Madrid, Spain
- Bilbao I Doc and SFF, Spain
- Curtacinema – Rio de Janeiro ISFF, Brazil
- European SFF Brest, France
- Foyle FF, Derry-Londonderry, UK

- interfilm ISFF, Berlin, Germany
- PÖFF Shorts – Black Knights FF, Tallinn, Estonia
- Rio de Janeiro ISFF, Brazil
- Winterthur ISFF, Switzerland

December

- BogoShorts - Bogotá SFF, Colombia
- Leuven ISFF, Belgium

Feature Film Festivals, which also show short films:

January

- Slamdance FF, UT, USA
- Sundance FF, UT, USA

February

- Berlinale – Berlin IFF, Germany
- Gothenburg IFF, Sweden
- Rotterdam IFF, Holland
- Santa Barbara IFF, CA, USA

March

- Ann Arbour FF, MI, USA
- Athens IFF, Greece
- Cartagena IFF, Colombia
- Cinequest F & VR F, San Jose, CA, USA
- Cleveland IFF, Ohio, USA
- Guadalajara IFF, Mexico
- SXSW ISFF, Austin, Texas, USA

April

- Bafici, Buenos Aires, Argentinia
- European Media Arts FF, Osnabrück, Germany
- Images F, Toronto, Canada
- San Francisco FF, CA, USA
- Tribeca FF, New York, USA

May

- Cannes IFF, France
- Indie Lisboa IFF, Portugal
- Seattle IFF, WA, USA

June

- Chicago Underground FF, IL, USA
- Edinburgh IFF, UK
- Karlovy Vary IFF, Czech Republic
- Moscow IFF, Russia
- Sydney FF, Australia

July

- Fantasia FF, Montreal, Canada
- Madrid IFF, Spain
- Melbourne IFF, Australia

August

- Flickers: Rhode Island IFF, RI, USA
- La Guarimba FF, Amantea, Italy
- Locarno FF, Schwitzerland
- Sarajevo FF, Bosnia and Herzegovina

September

- Atlantic IFF, Halifax, NS, Canada
- Calgary IFF, Canada
- Edmonton IFF, Canada
- Message to Man IFF, St. Petersburg, Russia
- New York FF, NY, USA
- San Sebastian FF, Spain
- Split IFF, Croatia
- Telluride FF, USA
- Toronto IFF, Canada
- Venice FF, Italy

October

- AFI Fest, Los Angeles, USA
- Austin FF, Texas, USA
- Busan IFF, South Korea
- Chicago IFF, IL, USA
- Hamptons IFF, New York, USA
- Molodist IFF, Kiev, Ukraine
- Nashville FF, Tennessee, USA
- New Cinema F, Montreal, Canada
- Warsaw FF, Poland

November

- Calgary Underground FF, Canada
- Cork IFF, Ireland
- Kassel Doc F, Germany
- L'Alternativa Independent FF, Barcelona, Spain
- Leeds IFF, UK
- New Orleans Film Festival, LA, USA
- Raindance FF, London, UK

- St. Louis IFF, MO, USA

December

- Singapore IFF, Singapore

In addition to these festivals, which usually accept a broad spectrum of short films, some festivals only allow specific genres or cover other filmmaking niches. The largest of these niches, to which entire festivals are dedicated, are animated film, documentary film, children's and youth film, as well as LGBT+ film. A few festivals are internationally known in these niches and would be great for a premiere.

Festivals for documentaries

March

- CPH:DOX, Kopenhagen, Denmark
- True/False FF, Columbia, Missouri, USA

April

- Hot Docs IFF, Toronto, Ontario, Canada

June

- Sheffield Doc/Fest, UK

July

- AFI Docs FF, Washington DC, USA
- DokuFest I Documentary and SFF, Priszren, Kosovo

- Leipzig IF for Documentary and Animated Film, Germany
- Visions du Réel, Nyon, Switzerland

November

- IDFA – I Documentary FF Amsterdam, Holland

Festivals for Animations:

February

- Anima – Brussels AFF, Brüssel, Belgium

May

- Animayo – IFF of A, Visual Effects, Video Games, Las Palmas de Gran canaria, Spain
- ITFS – Stuttgart F of Animated F, Germany

June

- Animafest Zagreb, Kroatien, July
- Anima Mundi – IAFF, Rio de Janeiro, Sao Paulo, Brazil
- Siggraph Computer AF, Los Angeles, CA, USA

August

- Hiroshima IAF, Hiroshima, Japan

September

- Ottawa IAF, Canada

October

- Animator: IAFF, Poznan, Poland
- Bucheon IAF, South Korea
- Chilemonos IAF, Santiago, Chile

November

- Anim'est – IAFF, Bukarest, Romania

If you are looking for other animation festivals, I can highly recommend this website: https://www.animation-festivals.com

Festivals for children and youth films
March

- New York I Children's FF, USA

July

- Giffoni FF, Giffoni Valle Piana, Italy

November

- Chicago I Children's FF, IL, USA
- Gijon IFF, Spain

Festivals with a focus on LGBT+:
March

- BFI Flare: London LGBTIQ+ FF, UK

June

- Mostra Fire!! De Cine LGBT De Barcelona, Spain

July

- Outfest Los Angeles LGBT Film Festival, CA, USA

September

- Frameline: The San Francisco I LGBT+ FF CA, USA
- Reeling: The Chicago LGBT+ IFF, IL, USA

Oktober

- ImageOut Rochester LGBT FF, NY, USA
- Mix Copenhagen, Denmark

Other festivals are highly regarded in their respective niches, such as the Sitges - Fantastic Film Festival of Catalonia (Spain) for the fantasy films, the Premier Plans Festival (Angers, France) for student films, and the Camerimage Film Festival (Bydgoszcz, Poland), which focuses on cine-matography.

* * *

IMPORTANT! These lists are aimed at the international market. Besides, several festivals are probably not crucial for this market but are highly respected in the countries where they are held. In Germany, for example, this would be the Max Ophüls Prize in Saarbrücken.

Many countries also award a national short film prize. In the

UK, for example, this is the British Academy Film Award. Of course, to receive a nomination or an award at those festivals would be an excellent start for your film too.

* * *

DON'T GET TOO ATTACHED to the big festivals like Cannes or Sundance. Often, less than one per cent of the submissions make it into the programs there. So statistically speaking, you have an extremely bad chance. Besides that, there are, as the list should show, so many other exciting festivals.

Of course, several interesting festivals will be added to these lists in the coming years. And there are just as many which are very new and unknown now, but which may be among the known ones in a few years. And perhaps you will have even better opportunities to get in contact with industry representatives at these smaller, manageable festivals. So don't wait too long for the promise of big festivals, because you will miss some nice opportunities.

HOW DO YOU SUBMIT TO FESTIVALS?

After choosing a few festivals for a possible film premiere, you have to submit your film to them. There are different ways to do this.

Firstly, you should of course look at the Rules and Regulations of the selected festivals. You can usually find them on their websites or on the submission platforms that festivals cooperate with. Don't throw your money away because your film does not meet their criteria.

Nowadays, most festivals prefer submissions via online platforms or their websites. In some cases, you can also submit by e-mail. But let's go step by step.

SUBMISSION PLATFORMS

Nowadays, almost all submissions take place online. The days of sending DVDs are over. Only a few people can remember the times when you had to drag VHS tapes, Beta cams, or even real film copies to the post office.

Various submission platforms have now established themselves as digital alternatives. FilmFreeway has been the most successful and has replaced the pioneer and long-time market leader WithoutaBox. WithoutaBox has now even ceased operations completely and other smaller platforms, such as Reelport, have been forced out of the market as well.

In addition to FilmFreeway, there are other providers you should take advantage of. Some of them supply other countries and festivals and offer interesting features that simplify the submission process for you. It is also important to counteract the market monopolization of FilmFreeway.

To submit your film to one of these platforms, you need a profile. This means that you type the most crucial information about the film into an interface and upload film stills, director's photos, and other additional material. You will then have to either upload your film to the platform in question or integrate it via a streaming link (for example, via Vimeo). This is initially free of charge.

After you have done that, you can choose one (or more) from the list of festivals the platform cooperates with and submit your film. The platform will then send the necessary information and your film to the festival.

A fee is usually charged for each submission. For short films, this fee is generally between 1.00 Euro and 3.00 Euro. Discount systems and subscriptions can reduce fees. Besides, many festivals charge a festival fee, especially the American ones.

It may well be that you feel overwhelmed by the sheer number of festivals presenting themselves on these platforms at the beginning. Don't be discouraged here. There are a few methods of getting an overview relatively quickly. But more about that later.

In the following, I have listed the submission platforms that are currently in use.

IMPORTANT! On some of these platforms, you can subscribe to a newsletter. After that, you will be bombarded with e-mails about festival deadlines. Don't let this influence you too much; stay with the festivals you have already chosen! Under no circumstances should you take notice of every deadline pointed out to you. Otherwise, you will be broke very quickly.

* * *

29

LIST OF SUBMISSION PLATFORMS

Currently, several submission platforms cooperate with different festivals. The most frequently used are:

• **FilmFreeway.** This platform was founded in Canada in 2014 and has quickly become the market leader, mainly because it was simply easier and cheaper for filmmakers to submit here than through the competitors. Likewise, film festivals had to pay less commission than on other platforms. FilmFreeway is also still the only provider that does not charge filmmakers a submission fee.

Within minutes, you can create a profile for you and your film and start sending your film to thousands of festivals. The focus is on English-speaking countries.

The sheer number of festivals (about 9,000) on this platform can be overwhelming, but some easy-to-use filters can bring some order to the chaos. You can sort the festivals by entry fees, countries, and other categories.

Website: www.filmfreeway.com

Submission fee: none

* * *

IMPORTANT! Repeatedly, I have come across so-called "fake" festivals. These are festivals that charge an entry fee, but never actually take place, or at least not in the way one would imagine a film festival taking place. FilmFreeway is aware of this problem and has announced stricter controls, but did not do much in the end. Since it is still very easy to pass yourself off as a festival here, you must continue to be careful on this platform and check that the festivals you submit to exist in fact.

* * *

• FESTHOME. FestHome was founded in Spain in 2010 and has many European, and especially Spanish speaking, festivals in its list. I like this platform and find the overviews and statistics about how your film is doing in different countries extremely helpful. There is a small fee per submission, but there are discounts and a very cheap annual pass for unlimited submissions above a certain number. For some time now, the service also offers an integrated VoD service as well as help with subtitling and DCP creation. It is also possible to send the screening copies directly via the platform.

Website: www.festhome.com

Submission fee: 2.00 € (more than 5 submissions 1.79 €, more than 20 submissions 1.50 €, more than 75 submissions 1.20 €. One year unlimited submissions are available for 49.95 €).

. . .

• **FILMFESTIVALLIFE (FFL)** IS a German platform that started as a search engine/database for film festivals in 2009 and eventually developed into a submission platform. The focus here is more on European festivals. A single submission is relatively expensive, but even here there are different plans to reduce the fees in the long run and, if you submit several, they are relatively cheap. The platform also tries to establish itself as a social network for filmmakers, and one can follow other submitters and their film careers.

Website: www.filmfestivallife.com

Submission fee: 2.99 € (for one month unlimited submission 5.00 €, for three months unlimited submission 13.50 €, for one-year unlimited submission 48.00 €).

• **SHORTFILMDEPOT** WAS FOUNDED in France in 2004 and focuses on renowned festivals (mainly European) and exclusively on short films. The festivals here are very clearly structured and are subject to extensive controls. Therefore, there is no black sheep on this platform. The most prominent festival on the site is the Clermont-Ferrand Short Film Festival, at which ShortFilmDepot was also founded. To submit your film, you first have to buy the platform's internal currency (stamps) and upload your film, which is a bit cumbersome.

Website: www.shortfilmdepot.com

Submission fee: 3.00 € (more than 5 submissions 2.50 € per submission, more than 20 submissions 1.95 € per submission, more than 75 submissions 1.50 € per submission, more than 400 submissions 0.50 € per submission).

. . .

• CLICKFORFESTIVALS IS a submission platform founded in 2013 by a well-known Spanish film distributor. There are consequently many Spanish language festivals in the catalogue. The fees are comparatively low. However, the platform is also limited to the absolute basics, and there are no other features, distribution statistics, etc. You can either upload your film here or use a Vimeo or Dropbox link.

Website: www.clickforfestivals.com

Fee per submission: 2.00 € (more than 5 submissions 1.80 € per submission, more than 10 submissions 1.70 € per submission, more than 20 submissions 1.60 € per submission, more than 50 submissions 1.50 € per submission, more than 75 submissions 1.40 € per submission, more than 100 submissions 1.20 € per submission, more than 200 submissions 1.00 € per submission).

• MOVIBETA IS another Spanish platform that exists since 2009. Here you can find mainly Spanish, Italian, and Latin American festivals. The website is, unfortunately, quite rudimentary, yet is accessible in many languages. Even here, you can find some festivals that do not appear on other sites. So it might be worthwhile to create an account here as well.

Website: www.movibeta.com

Submission fee: 4.84 € (more than 3 submissions 4.66 € per submission, more than 5 submissions 4.00 € per submission, more than 10 submissions 3.00 € per submission, more than 20 submissions 2.00 € per submission, more than 40 submissions 1.50 € per submission)

• FILMFEST PLATFORM. FilmFest Platform is a French platform and cooperates mainly with French-speaking festivals. Unfortunately, French people usually speak only French. That's why you need French subtitles here if your film's original language is different. But if you have them, it might be worthwhile to submit your film via the FilmFest Platform, because many of the festivals listed here are only accessible via this platform. Of course, this also applies to films without dialogue.

Website: www.filmfestplatform.com

Submission fee: 2.90 € (more than 5 submissions 2.80 € per submission, more than 10 submissions 2.50 € per submission, more than 50 submissions 1.50 € per submission).

* * *

TIP: A few festivals prefer submissions via their website or don't offer any other options at all. Be careful not to miss these festivals. Your chances are much better here since many filmmakers nowadays focus exclusively on submissions via online platforms.

* * *

IMPORTANT! The digital world is subject to constant and rapid change. A submission platform that was popular yesterday may be replaced by a new one tomorrow. For example, three major platforms (WithoutaBox, Reelport, UptoFest) recently closed their doors almost simultaneously. The information and recommendations given are as of winter of 2020.

* * *

30

A FEW MORE TIPS TO MAKE IT INTO
THE PROGRAM OF POPULAR FESTIVALS

S ubmit as early as possible. Festivals usually try to screen all submitted films and offer all filmmakers equal opportunities. However, around the deadline, a flood of films usually deluges the curators. And that's exactly when the viewing time becomes very short. At some point, the deadline arrives, and the program has to stand. It can happen that the curator, when it's your film's turn, has already been running a film marathon for hours or days and possibly has just stuck matches between his eyelids. In contrast, the same curator having received a submission previously, may be lying on the couch relaxing, enjoying his evening off by watching your film. Perhaps your film is the only one he sees that evening. In other words, the earlier you submit, the more likely your film will receive the curator's undivided attention.

Besides, it is often much cheaper to submit early. Many festivals have different deadlines, such as the Early Bird Deadline, Regular Deadline, Late Deadline, and sometimes the Very Late Deadline. And the entry fees vary according to the unofficial policy: the earlier, the cheaper. The intention is to encourage filmmakers to submit early and to prevent hell from breaking loose shortly before the deadline.

So, by submitting early, you not only increase the chances of your film being viewed attentively, but you will also pay a lot less in fees.

• **In case of doubt, please submit.** You can never know with one hundred percent certainty what the curators like, or what the main themes of the respective festivals (and film blocks) will be this year. Sure, you can and should get an idea of the programmers' merits by looking through previous years' festival programs. But if there is even a hint of indecision afterwards as to whether you should submit or not, I advise you to submit. I have already experienced so many positive surprises with this approach.

• **Keep your website up-to-date.** Make sure your website and other sites on the Internet that mention the film or team members are up to date. If the curators like your film, the next step, besides a look at the press kit, is usually a short online research. Outdated or even wrong information makes an awful impression here. In contrast, an appealing and up-to-date online presence or a large follow-up community in social networks could increase your chances of acceptance.

• **Keep the information on the submission platforms up-to-date.** Be thorough and accurate. The more fields you fill out at FilmFreeway and Co., the more information is available to the festivals. Often these materials can be crucial to the game. The festival vita in particular should always be up to date. Many curators note where the film has already been shown. This information then flows consciously, or subconsciously, into the decision for or against a film.

Festivals want to get their halls full. If you show them at the time of submission that they can promote your film, the chances of making it into the program increase. A strong synopsis, fancy posters, a captivating trailer, well-known actors, a large team, many festival successes, all of this increases the chances of acceptance.

• **Don't be discouraged.** Did you receive a rejection from a big festival? Drink a coffee and submit your film somewhere else!

Over the years, I have often seen filmmakers give up too early, even though they have produced some impressive films that could have had an exciting festival career. Even at the distribution company I worked for, it often happened that we had to encourage filmmakers to keep submitting. Often these films became enormously successful as a result. Therefore, I strongly advise you not to bury your head in the sand too quickly.

It often takes a while for a film to get its first approval, which may not augur badly much at first. It especially need not be that the quality of your film is bad. You will see that once this first confirmation is received, other festivals will join in much faster.

31

WHAT TO DO IF YOUR FILM IS NOT ACCEPTED?

I t can be painful to open your e-mail box and find a festival rejection in there. Should that happen, it is important to behave professionally. If you as an artist cannot deal with rejections of this kind and rejections in general in a healthy way, you will have a tough time in the future. So please don't answer all offended or insulted by these rejections. Please don't write back that the festival has made the biggest mistake since its existence, or even start insulting the curators. Remember: you *always* run into each other twice.

Simply delete the rejection e-mail instead. Out of sight, out of mind. Remember that most festivals can show less than five per cent of the films submitted. There is no reason to be offended. Maybe there was a theme this year that your film did not fit. Or there were too many submissions from your country. Or too many films with the same theme. Whatever the reason, the festival most likely did not decide against your film (and certainly not against you), but simply for another one. So stay calm, delete the e-mail, and keep submitting.

* * *

TIP: Of course, you are interested in the reason for the rejection of your film. How could this happen? You are welcome to send this question back. But the chance of getting an answer is tiny.

On the one hand, this is probably because there is no one clear answer to the question. If your film was not selected, it does not necessarily mean that there is something wrong with it, but rather that the curators liked other films better. Or that those others fit better into the program.

On the other hand, the festival organizers have the least time to respond to you around the time of the rejection. They are in the final stages of the festival preparations and are already working overtime anyway. So if you want to increase your chances of getting feedback, I would advise you to follow up later. Preferably, a few weeks after the festival has taken place.

* * *

32

WHEN SHOULD YOU GIVE UP
SUBMITTING TO FESTIVALS?

M aybe one rejection e-mail after the other will arrive in the beginning. And so it may occur to you to ask yourself what sense further submissions would make.

I can only advise you here repeatedly not to be discouraged too quickly. The nature of making submissions to festivals is that the chances of rejection are simply very high.

But if you are receiving one rejection after the other without a single invitation, *then* you should check a few things:

1.) Is the screener playable? Firstly, you should confirm that your film is playable at all. In other words, check whether the festival screener can be played correctly. If you are submitting via Vimeo, you should also ensure that all settings are correct (see the chapter "The most important Vimeo settings").

2.) Are all details correct? Then you should check if all the information you entered in the submission platforms displays correctly, or whether anything important is missing. For example, if you have typed in the wrong date of production like one too far in the past, it can be a reason for rejection.

3.) Check the spam folder of your e-mail inbox. Sometimes festivals send out the invitation e-mails directly via the submission platforms. These also quickly end up in the spam folder.

4.) Are all e-mail notifications activated on the submission platforms? From time to time, festivals communicate their selections exclusively via the submission platforms. However, if you have deactivated the corresponding options, your film may be shown at a festival without anyone informing you.

5.) Arrange the rejections in their context. What festivals have you submitted to so far? And how many? Have you only submitted to festivals that *every* filmmaker dreams of entering?

Then maybe it is time to spread the submissions more widely. If it simply doesn't work out with the huge or well-known festivals, submit to medium-sized or small ones. Only when you have submitted to 50 - 100 film festivals of various sizes will you be able to draw firm conclusions about the festival potential of your film.

But if you have already received more than 60 rejections from various festivals and still haven't received a single confirmation, then it might be time to think about other distribution channels. These could be online releases, for example. Just because festivals have rejected your film doesn't mean it won't be successful on Vimeo or become a viral hit on YouTube.

33

CAN YOUR FILM BE SUCCESSFUL EVEN IF YOU CANNOT AFFORD THE FESTIVAL FEES?

I deally, filmmakers should set aside a small portion of their budget for the distribution even before production. But this usually (and unfortunately) does not happen very often in reality. Most of the time, they are left without any money after the shoot, or are even in debt.

If you belong to the latter group, you might ask yourself the question: Can my film be successful if I can't afford the expensive submission fees?

Here I can calm you down. The answer is yes. On the one hand, many exciting festivals around the world require little or no entry fee. Among them are even some of the most important short film festivals globally, such as Clermont-Ferrand. On the other hand, there are also ways to circumvent the fees or get discounts. I will come to that in the next chapter.

Also, your distribution budget might unexpectedly increase during the distribution. For example, you might win an award or sell your film to a broadcaster.

In summary, a large distribution budget is beneficial, but not an absolute must, at least not in the short film sector. Some of the most successful short films of recent years have established themselves almost exclusively through festivals that charged little or no fees.

34

HOW DO YOU AVOID THE FESTIVAL FEE?

I n the USA in particular, festivals often demand very high entry fees, which many filmmakers cannot afford. If you are among this number, you need not become dejected, because there are a few ways to submit your film anyway. In many cases, it is possible to ask for a so-called Fee Waiver. The best way to do this is to send a short e-mail.

But before you begin asking every festival for a fairy waiver, I must briefly point out that festivals usually have a good reason to ask for a submission fee. Festivals also incur high costs, which ticket sales alone generally cannot cover. Consequently, in Europe many festivals enjoy state support. Unfortunately, this is not the case in other countries, such as the USA. So it is far from being the case that festivals grant Fee Waivers to anyone who asks for them. They can't afford that. Therefore, it would help if you gave good reasons why you and your film deserve a fee waiver. Please do not stray too far from reality here.

Typical reasons that could lead to a festival waiving all or part of the entry fee include those following. The more of these that apply, the better.

• **Poor production country.** If you submit your film from a country that is in a relatively low economic situation, there is a good chance that the fee will be waived. It is not fair or understandable that filmmakers from Switzerland, for example, have to pay the same festival submission fee as their colleagues from Bangladesh. Many festivals acknowledge this by supporting filmmakers from financially weaker countries with Fee Waivers. If on top of everything else, your country suffers from sanctions that make financial transactions more difficult, as is the case in Iran, for example, you have a good chance of getting a full Fee Waiver.

• **Regular guest.** If you have already been a guest at a festival with your film, it might be worthwhile to ask for a waiver of fees the next time you submit your film. After all, film festivals love to see filmmakers come back. It is best if you are still in contact with the festival's staff. Then you could write to them directly and let them know that you have finished a new film. Send the press kit and offer to forward a Vimeo link. Most likely, the festival will respond and you will avoid the fees.

• **Film Student.** Additionally, as a film student, you have the chance to get a Fee Waiver or at least a reduction of the submission fees. But here you have to make a little more effort in formulating your demand. It is not enough to be just a film student, as there are students out there who could easily afford to pay the fees. Some of them are even supported by their university. So you should briefly explain why this is not the case for you and why you cannot afford the festival fees. Besides, it is always advisable to explain your motivation for submitting to this particular festival.

• **Suitable film theme.** Often festivals focus on a specific theme or country. Maybe you are lucky, and your film fits that. For example, if you have found out that a festival is planning a focus for the next edition in the country where your film is set, chances are that your submission will be made easier. Good research can be worth its weight in gold here, in the truest sense of the word.

• **Successful film.** Curators enjoy showing films that have caused an international sensation. This is also an advertisement for the festivals. If they can announce that there are short film gems in the program, such as films shown in Cannes or nominated for an Oscar, the audience is attracted, as well as the press. If your film belongs to this top of the short film pyramid, you should advertise your past successes and ask for a Fee Waiver.

The best way to do this is to write an e-mail to the festivals and let them know that you have a short film that could fit well into their program and that has already been very successful. You should then list the film's greatest successes and refer to the press kit and the festival vita that you attached to the e-mail. Then you should note that you cannot afford to submit any more films at the moment, and ask if the festival could accommodate you with a Fee Waiver. The more successful your film was, the higher your chances to arouse the organisers' curiosity.

Incidentally, it is also common for curators to study the programs of major festivals, and then, on their initiative, write to the filmmakers and offer a free submission for their festival. This is either because they are curious about these films or because they hope to enhance their program.

• **Known names.** The same thing that applies to a successful film applies to one in which so-called VIPs have participated.

So if you were able to win Gérard Depardieu for your short film, this has extreme advertising potential. I am sure that you will get many fee waivers and many commitments even if the film is only mediocre.

However, the VIPs listed by you must be known in the country where the festival takes place.

• **Interesting film project.** If the points listed so far do not apply to your film or you, you might be able to pull one last wild card out of your sleeve: the film itself. Is there a unique selling point that makes it stand out from the crowd in a way that would enrich a festival program? Maybe you have succeeded in creating something exciting, novel, or politically explosive; then, *that's* what you have to communicate.

In a short e-mail, you will explain why the film could fit so perfectly into the respective festival programs. You might have a synopsis, a press kit, or a trailer that has the potential to make curators curious. Attach it. You have to formulate succinctly why your film would bring significant value to the festival. Why does it fit into the festival program like a fist in the eye? Why will the audience love the film? These should be expressed in the most enthusiastic (but not pushy) way possible.

This method is undoubtedly the least promising. But, if you have created something very unique, it could pay off.

* * *

TIP: The earlier you ask, the higher your chances of receiving. Some festivals only allocate a certain contingent of Fee Waivers. And in the days and weeks shortly before the deadline (when the festival is flooded with films) the chance of being allowed to submit free of charge is tiny.

* * *

IMPORTANT! In any case, you should keep your e-mails short. Festivals get many requests of this kind. So keep it as short as possible, be polite, and get to the point quickly. If you make a request that takes a lot of time to read, you are only demonstrating your inexperience.

But it would help if you also avoid the impression of a mass e-mail. Therefore, it is better to write to the curators directly and personally. It would be best if you could also say a few words about the festival.

35

WHAT IS A COVER LETTER AND DO YOU NEED IT?

O n the submission platforms you sometimes have the opportunity to send a cover letter with the submission, in which you explain why you are submitting to this particular festival.

A cover letter can dramatically increase your chances of being accepted. But only if you manage to give convincing reasons why your film is a good fit for that festival program. These could be, for example, the following:

• **Your film fits the theme.** Perhaps you will submit to a festival that offers a side series on a specific subject or theme, within which you feel your film could fit perfectly. Or the whole focus of the festival is on the topic your film is about. Then it might be worth mentioning it in the cover letter.

• **The festival has shown films by you in the past.** Maybe, at one of the last editions of the festival, a film of yours was shown. The positive memories are the reason why you would like to revisit this festival; mention that in the cover letter.

Festivals want to keep in touch with their guests from past years and are happy about loyal, returning filmmakers.

• **You have personal reasons.** Maybe the festival is recommended by someone who has been there before. Or you have another personal reason why you would like to show your film at this very festival, in this very city or country. Then why not explain this to the festival in the cover letter?

IMPORTANT! Copy-and-paste-spam produces the opposite effect! Before you attach a cover letter to your submission, you should have researched that festival in detail. It's best to address the curator directly. Write a cover letter only if you have convincing reasons; otherwise, it will leave a rather bland aftertaste.

* * *

36

WHAT HAPPENS AFTER THE FILM HAS BEEN ACCEPTED BY A FESTIVAL?

H ere it is, at last, the first festival selection. You have received an invitation by e-mail, and a warm, *great* feeling comes over you. Enjoy it. Nobody can take this success away from you! From now on, you have the opportunity to advertise with this official selection. But more importantly, you can add an event to your calendar that will hopefully bring you a lot of positive experiences and, in the best case, boost your career.

After you have received the invitation, you should take care of several things. First, you need all the essential information about the festival. When will the festival take place? And where? Is your film in the official competition or a side program? Does the film festival pay a screening fee? Is it able to pay for accommodation and travel?

Usually, you will receive this information directly with your selection by e-mail. If not, ask.

In any case, you should not take too much time to respond to the invitation. And it is recommended to accept the invitation or withdraw from the festival relatively quickly. Often it is enough to write a short e-mail back, including accompanying material and screening copies, and tell them how happy you are about the acceptance. Sometimes the festivals also expect you to fill out a form or sign a document confirming that you own all film rights.

Of course, you should share the great news with your team as soon as possible. They will thank you for keeping them up to date. It also happens from time to time that festivals can host several team members and maybe even pay for their travel expenses. For example, festivals often like to have the actors on-site, next to the director.

* * *

IMPORTANT! Read the invitation carefully. Often a few deadlines are included with it. Usually, these are the dates by which you should have confirmed your participation, by when the festival needs the additional material, and when the screening copy should be available. You can usually miss these deadlines for some days, but doing so will make you unpopular quickly. In the worst case, you run the risk of your film's removal from the program. Some festivals have become allergic to filmmakers who do not fulfil their duties or do not read the instructions.

* * *

DO FILM FESTIVALS PAY FOR ACCOMMODATION AND TRAVEL?

M ost festivals attach great importance to the personal presence of filmmakers. Therefore, there is often a budget available to make this possible.

Often, festivals can offer a few nights in a hotel or arrange accommodation with residents. Sometimes they are also able to cover the travel costs.

So if you are interested in attending a festival, you should check to see if you can count on support—no false modesty at this point. The festivals usually get many requests of this kind. That's why they typically have clear guidelines and will be able to give you information quickly.

CAN YOU CHARGE A SCREENING FEE FOR YOUR SHORT FILM?

In principle, screening fees are paid much less frequently for short films than for feature films - unfortunately. But some festivals can afford to pay short filmmakers for screening their work. Therefore, it can be worthwhile to ask for a screening fee. However, there are a few things to consider.

WHEN DO YOU ASK FOR A SCREENING FEE?

You can always ask for a screening fee. I think it is entirely legitimate for you as a filmmaker to take care of your work payment. You don't have to be ashamed of that.

In general, however, the chances of earning fees are very small, at least if your film is running in a competition where there is prize money on offer. Here you will most often receive a friendly rejection and be informed that your film has a chance to win much more than a screening fee.

However, if your work is shown in programs, besides the main competition, things will look quite different. Since you have no chance of winning an award and because out-of-competition performances are usually less prestigious, many festivals are willing to pay a small fee here. Your chances are particularly high if the festival itself has invited your film to the side program without you submitting it before.

* * *

TIP: Over the years, I have noticed that the so-called niche festivals are much more willing to pay screening fees than the more diversified festivals. For example, it is common in the LGBT+ sector to pay a fee for screening short films.

HOW DO YOU ASK FOR A SCREENING FEE?

The best way to find out is to use the e-mail you send in response to the selection notification. Just ask in a side sentence if the festival can pay a screening fee. Make sure this doesn't sound too demanding and don't forget to express your delight about the invitation. You will get a quick and usually friendly response.

41

WHAT CAN YOU CHARGE AS A
SCREENING FEE FOR A SHORT FILM?

The amount of the screening fee depends on various factors, like the film's running time. For a 45-minute film, you can logically charge more than for a 5-minute film. Also, the size of the festival and the audience will affect the pricing. How many paying guests will attend? Additionally, it depends on how many times the film will be shown. Some festivals will only show your film once; others will screen the same program on different days in diverse locations. Last but not least, it also depends a bit on the country where the festival is held.

On average, the fee for screening a short film at a festival is around 40.00 Euro to 80.00 Euro (including taxes). But some festivals can pay a screening fee of 200.00 Euro or more. And of course, many basically cannot afford a screening fee.

HOW DO YOU RECEIVE THE SCREENING FEES?

Once you have agreed with a festival on the fee amount, you will generally be asked to submit an invoice. It's best to send this as soon as possible, by e-mail. The flat fee negotiated with festivals is usually inclusive of taxes or other applicable costs.

* * *

IMPORTANT! Screening fees can only be charged by the actual owner of the film rights. If you made the film as a student, you would need permission from your college or university.

* * *

43

CAN YOU WITHDRAW YOUR SHORT FILM FROM A FESTIVAL AFTER YOU RECEIVE AN INVITATION?

I can succinctly answer this question: Yes, you have the right to withdraw your film even after a festival has selected it. Theoretically. But this is understandably not very welcome among festivals, and you should only do it if there are very good reasons for it. After all, with the submission, you've entered into a kind of contract, and the festival has taken the trouble to evaluate your film. Most importantly, the festival has already put together a program, and the film is now a fixed part of it. Despite all this, there may be a few reasons that speak against a screening. These would be, for example, the following:

• **Premiere status.** Sometimes, you receive a selection from several festivals, and these festivals demand the same premiere status. So, for example, you receive a selection from two festivals in New York at the same time, and both festivals would like your film to have its New York premiere at their venue. Or, after you receive a selection, you want to wait for a selection (or rejection) from another festival because that festival requires premiere status. So you may be forced to cancel one festival to reserve the premiere for another.

* * *

TIP: It may also happen that you receive an invitation from one festival, but are still waiting for the selection (or rejection) of another festival with which there could be a premiere conflict. In this case, it would make sense for you to inquire about the latter's status quickly. To do so, you should write to the festival and tell them that you have just received a selection from another festival, but would prefer to premiere at theirs. Then ask if your film has been watched and if anyone can give you early information about the chances. Most festivals will answer you willingly and quickly, as they know this problem. They may also be flattered that you are choosing their festival over the competition.

* * *

• SUPPORTING SERIES. It may happen that your film has been invited into an out-of-competition program. This often eliminates the chance for prize money. Also, these side series are very often less attended than the competition programs. However, since you originally submitted for the competition, it is of course legitimate to withdraw your film in this case if you do not find this new programming interesting enough.

However, do not act too hastily. Often these side programs are very popular and well-attended events too. Sometimes it is also possible to win awards there, such as audience awards. And sometimes screening fees are paid for these programs. Moreover, screening in a side program is usually still worth more than no screening at all, especially if it's a well-attended festival.

• **Unfinished.** Your film isn't finished after all, or you don't have all the rights you need for screening. Maybe you decided to go back to the editing room and make a few more changes. Or you didn't manage to get permission for a song title you used. Then you don't have much choice but to pull your movie back.

IF ANY OF these reasons apply to your situation and you want or need to withdraw your film, I would let the festival know as soon as possible. In the e-mail, you should briefly describe why you are withdrawing your film. Then you can offer to show it next year instead.

In my many years in short film distribution, it has happened from time to time that we have had to withdraw a short film. The vast majority of festivals have been highly understanding and cooperative. Often they have agreed to show the film the next year.

* * *

IMPORTANT! At some point, festivals print programs, hold press conferences, and post their programs online. So if you want to withdraw your film, you should do it as soon as possible after an acceptance. This will save you and the festival a lot of stress.

44

WHAT KIND OF SCREENING COPIES DO
YOU NEED?

Most festivals require a DCP (Digital Cinema Package) or a high-resolution film file, such as a MOV file (preferably Apple ProRes 422 HQ, 48 kHz, 24-bit audio) or an MP4 file (H.264, 48 kHz, 24-bit audio). If you can offer your movie in these three formats, preferably with and without English subtitles, you should be good to go.

• **DCP.** I would advise you to have the DCP done by a professional post-production house. This will probably save you a lot of time and headaches. But if that doesn't fit your budget, you can also create it yourself relatively easily. You can do it free of charge with the freeware DCP-o-Matic or a bit more complicated with OpenDCP. I have used these programs for my films and can recommend them. More and more editing programs now also offer a DCP export option, but the results are often not satisfactory.

* * *

ACHTUNG: Please do not protect the DCP with a KDM

(Key Delivery Message). This will only cause unnecessary hassle for you and the festival, and it is not welcome in the short film business.

* * *

SOME FESTIVALS now also work with partners who offer conversion at a reasonable price. Or, if you are lucky, there is someone at the festival who will create a DCP for you. However, this is rare, and mostly it's up to you to meet the festivals' format requirements.

• **MOV and MP4.** Many festivals, especially in the short film sector, are technically not able to screen DCPs. I guess that at present, the majority of festivals still prefer other file formats. The most popular formats are definitely .mov (best Apple ProRes 422 HQ encoding) and .mp4 (also with an H.264 encoding). Ideally, you can deliver both formats. So one MOV and one MP4 file with 1920 x 1080 resolution and audio stereo mix.

If you want to send other formats, such as a file encoded with Avid DNxHD, I would advise you first to ask the festival if it makes sense to bother.

* * *

IMPORTANT! I advise you to test the screening copies you are sending thoroughly, preferably in a cinema. Many projectionists are very cooperative here. The festivals also check the screening copies before the festival starts, but usually only in excerpts. So if you want to guarantee that the picture and sound are up to your expectations over the entire length of the film, you should check it yourself.

* * *

YOU SHOULD ALSO MEET the format requirements of the respective film festivals. Very few festivals have the capacity or know-how to convert films themselves. So if you send the wrong format, you will probably be asked to send a suitable one eventually. If things go badly, the request will come just a few days before the festival starts. And if it goes really badly, there will be no request at all, and you will be in for a nasty surprise at the screening.

* * *

TIP: It's also best to upload the screening copies to a cloud of your choice, so that you only have to forward the download links and don't have to upload the entire film again with every acceptance. Especially later in your film's career, when you sometimes receive several selections in a week, you save yourself a lot of work this way.

* * *

45

HOW DO YOU SEND YOUR FILM TO THE FESTIVAL?

Feature films are usually sent on hard drives. However, short films are increasingly being transmitted on USB sticks or online (via data transfer or download link).

• **Hard drive or USB media.** If you are sending a USB stick, it is best to format it so that DCP servers can recognize it, in FAT32, or even better Linux Extended-2 or 3. FAT32 is unfortunately limited to 4 GB and is therefore not always suitable. If your film needs more memory and you can't (or don't want to) format it to Linux, you can also send it on a USB stick formatted in another way. Festivals often ignore this, because they have several ways to copy the movies themselves. But it can also happen that your stick can't be read if you send it with Mac OS X or NTFS formatting.

* * *

TIP: Send 3.0. USB sticks and not 2.0. After the festival, you usually get the data medium back free of charge.

* * *

• **SERVER UPLOAD.** Many festivals want you to upload your film to a server of their choice. This requires a fast and stable internet connection. Should you get several selections simultaneously, such uploads can become very time- and energy-consuming for you. Offering download links would be a more straightforward approach at this point. Try it. Most festivals accept those.

• **Partner services of the festivals.** A few companies take care of technical compliance on behalf of the festivals. In that case, the festival will ask you to send your film to one of these companies. They will then check whether the film complies with the festival's guidelines. If it does, it will be forwarded. If not, you will be asked to submit a new file, or receive an offer to convert your film into the desired format for a fee.

* * *

ATTENTION! Be careful here. You should be aware that these providers make their money mainly by converting movies. I have often experienced that these festival partners quickly find a reason why your already created DCP does not meet the guidelines. For example, you are told that a subtitle is not precisely in the image's designated area. They will then offer to create a new DCP. And that will cost you, of course.

Please don't misunderstand; I don't want to discredit all these providers. Most of them do a good job. I just want to give a little warning, as I have had various experiences with them myself.

* * *

• DOWNLOAD LINK. This is the best option for you as a film-maker. You only have to upload the movie to a cloud once and then you can just forward a download link. It's also ultimately the fastest and most energy-efficient method, and - I hope - the one that will prevail in the long run. At least in the short film sector.

So I would always try to offer the download link to the festivals first. Only when they insist on another option would I comply with those requests.

Besides the clouds, there are also services, such as WeTransfer or MyAirbridge, which are great for sending larger files. However, here the download links are only available for a certain amount of time, and you have to keep re-uploading the videos.

* * *

IMPORTANT! No matter which cloud option you choose, it makes sense to keep your DCP files together in an archive (for example .zip or .rar). Otherwise, there is a risk that the file structure will be destroyed by the cloud provider and will be unusable after the upload. But please also make sure that the file is not compressed.

* * *

AFTER YOU RECEIVE A SELECTION E-MAIL, you can make it easy for yourself and the festival by sending everything requested directly and in one go. This means that you accept the invitation, send the additional material, as well as a set of screening copies, and attach signed contracts if applicable. Such an e-mail might read as follows:

Dear Festival Team,

Thank you so much for the great news! We are pleased that our film TITLE has been selected for the next edition of your festival. That is very exciting. I will mark the event in my calendar. Are you going to pay a screening fee?

Additional material

Please find here a link to download the press kit (synopsis, biography of the director, festival vita ...), a photo of the director, the time-coded transcripts, as well as some high-resolution stills: download link

Screening Copy

Please find below the screening formats that I have available now:

DCP, Engl. ST.: download link

ProRes 422 HQ, Engl. ST (Stereo), 25fps: download link

MP4, H.264, Engl. ST, 1080P, 25 fps: download link

If you need anything else or if you have any questions do not hesitate to contact me!

Thank you again! I am looking forward to hearing from you.

All the best,

David M. Lorenz

- **Emergency backup option - Vimeo link.** Another safety measure for you is always have the Vimeo access data to your film, i.e. the link and the password, at hand. This option has often proven to be a handy emergency solution for me. For example, if a festival on the other side of the world suddenly has trouble playing the screening copies you sent out, you can simply forward that link as a backup. If you have activated the download option on Vimeo, the festival can then decide for itself which file it downloads and in which size. Vimeo offers a wide variety of versions here on its own. Sure, the screening quality will suffer, but it's still better than not screening the film at all.

46

A SHORT FESTIVAL SURVIVAL GUIDE

Okay, you've accepted the festival's invitation and sent out the additional materials and screening copies. Then it's a matter of making your trip as effective and fun as possible. To do this, I have a few ideas:

1.) Plan in detail. The first thing you should do is to plan your trip to the festival and organize your stay. At least a little bit. Because one thing is for sure: Once you are there, you won't have time for research.

That's why it's worth taking a look at the program before the festival. This is usually available online weeks in advance. For example, you should make a note of the screening times of your film. And it's best to make notes about other films and events that interest you.

It will pay off if you know which program points you want to participate in before you arrive. This will provide you with a common thread to follow as you make your way through stirring film presentations and Q&As, exciting discussions, inspiring new acquaintances, long all-nighters, and esca-lating film parties.

Alongside this, of course, you should organize travel and arrange accommodation. Also, make a note of the names and phone numbers of your local contacts.

TIP: Even if the invitation is silent on accommodation and travel, it can be worthwhile to ask about it politely. Very often, you will get some kind of support here.

2.) Get an overview. When you arrive at the festival, you should try to get a first impression as soon as possible. Who are your contacts? Where are the cinemas or event locations? When will the opening event take place?

Of course, it is also essential to find out as soon as possible when your film will be shown and whether there will be a Q&A session afterwards (or before). And whether there are any other appointments such as a previous talk with the presenters before your film's screening.

Most of the time, though, it's made very easy for you to gather this information, and you'll be greeted with a goodie bag upon arrival, including a map of the city and program booklet.

3.) Participate in workshops or other events. Often festi-vals offer exciting seminars or networking events. It is nearly always worthwhile to take advantage of these offers. Not only because you have the chance to learn something or get inspired, but also because you can meet and network with other filmmakers in attendance. Tailored to you as part of the target audience, these programs may well broaden your horizons.

4.) Watch all the screenings of your film. Even if there isn't going to be a Q&A about your film, it may be worth it to sit down in the theatre and watch the audience's reactions. It's merely one of the most exciting moments at film festivals when the lights go down, and the fruits of your labour are projected on the screen.

* * *

TIP: Bring a back-up copy of your film to the screening. Sure, usually everything should go fine (and most often does) because screening copies are tested beforehand. But every now and then something goes wrong, and suddenly your film has no sound, breaks halfway through, or is mixed up with another. I have experienced this many times. In such situations, it can be valuable if you have other screening options with you. In the meantime, try to stay as calm as possible. Please don't start barking at the projectionists or even insulting the festival organizers. This does no one any good and ultimately reflects poorly on you. By the way, the most professional reaction would be an apology from you to the audience.

* * *

5.) Talk to the festival guests. I can only advise you to talk to the guests after the screenings. It can be fascinating and eye opening to get feedback from the audience. Take the opportunity to make contacts here as well.

6.) Check out the other films. A festival is simply a great way to see what fellow filmmakers around the world are producing. This can be extremely informative about what the zeitgeist is right now, on the one hand, and merely entertaining or inspiring, on the other. It can also give you a sense of the tastes of the festival organizers. This could be interesting for future submissions.

7.) Get to know the other guests at the festival. Try to get to know the other filmmakers. Often they are at a similar stage in their careers, and exciting conversations can quickly ensue. The contacts you make at festivals can last well into your career and help shape it. Depending on the event's size, there may be representatives from other festivals in attendance or potential film distributors.

* * *

TIP: The most common question asked at film festivals (besides where did you get the idea from) is, what are you going to do next? It often happens that after the screening of your film, you'll be asked about it in the Q&A session. But even in personal conversations, the question about future artistic plans is an evergreen. So it can be worthwhile to come up with a small, effective pitch for your next project. You just never know when you might run into a prospective sponsor or collaborator.

* * *

8.) Promote your film. The main reason you're at a festival is probably to promote your film. So don't shy away from telling people about it! That's what film festivals are all about. Be prepared to pitch your film, preferably concisely and entertainingly. And as often as possible so that the auditorium will be full at your screening.

* * *

TIP: It's best to have a business card with you that includes a Vimeo link to your film. I've been happy every time filmmakers have handed me their films directly with their contacts.

* * *

9.) Behave decently and smile a lot. By the way, this is an excellent basic attitude for any situation in life. Remember that you are a guest. Be polite, or better - super friendly to the organizers. There is no need to make derogatory comments about other films or filmmakers. You also don't need to bitch about the festival location or the place where the festival takes place. It will all reflect negatively on you in the end. If you want to get these things off your chest, save them for your life partner or friends when you get back home.

Even if someone in the audience rips your film apart or the presenter asks a critical question, try to keep your composure. Don't let them provoke you or force you to satisfy their baser instincts. Swallow your ego and answer in a factual and friendly way. The festival scene is not as big as it sometimes seems, and festivals are well connected. Even though directors often have a reputation for being difficult, short film festivals, in particular, don't cater to this type of filmmaker.

10.) Join the parties. The film parties at many festivals are legendary. Besides the possibility to party extensively and usually spectacularly, you also have good opportunities to make new friends there. So, even if the day was exhausting, drag yourself there!

11.) Enjoy it. This is probably the most i-mportant. If, in addition to your professional duties, you manage to keep enjoying the festival to the fullest, then you've done everything right. Don't get too bogged down in taking care of business exclusively. Otherwise, you will miss too much. You should also have fun. Lots of it! Some of the most beautiful and exciting moments of my life have been at film festivals. And those were mostly moments when any business thoughts or film discussions were far away.

12.) Give thanks. Festival organizers are naturally pleased when what they've worked on for months is well received. So if you enjoyed the festival, express that in some way. Thank them for inviting you and give them feedback. If you had a good time, share that. Also, short thank you messages after the event, via e-mail or social media, are always well received.

13.) Keep in touch. You probably met a few filmmakers or other industry representatives at the festival that you liked. Maybe you collected business cards, or exchanged Facebook or other social media contacts. Be sure to keep in touch. This is very easy to do nowadays, especially via social media.

THE FESTIVAL RUN

As soon as the film premiere is set, the next phase of distribution begins. Now it's essential to submit to more festivals as quickly as possible, so that the film gets around and there isn't too big a gap in time between the premiere and the next screenings. Once the first official screening has taken place, the film is released and the clock is ticking. After all, a short film usually has a shelf life of two short years. After that, at least as far as festivals are concerned, its time is up and hardly anyone will want to show it. That's unfortunate, but a fact of life at the moment.

WHICH FESTIVALS SHOULD FOLLOW THE WORLD PREMIERE AND WHEN?

Of course, after the world premiere, you should continue to focus on submitting to established festivals. Ideally, you'll manage to get more prestigious festivals to follow the international premiere.

But you should also start now to spread out a bit and submit the film to mid-sized festivals and a bit later to smaller festivals so that there is not too big a gap in the film's vita. My advice is to start sending your film also to the festivals that either require a country premiere, only accept productions from the last year or have been running for a few years. In my opinion, the festival edition is a useful indicator at this stage of distribution to separate the wheat from the chaff. Especially if you don't have much distribution experience yet, you can use this number as a helpful guide.

Submit first to festivals that have been around for at least seven years. Of course, this number seems a bit out of the air now, and I don't want to discredit younger festivals with this 7th edition rule of thumb. Many very dedicated festivals simply haven't had the chance to establish themselves yet and need your support. There is nothing wrong with submitting to these festivals either, but I would wait a bit before doing so. Besides, there are now many festivals, and some kind of selection is necessary. The dividing lines have to be drawn somewhere. And I think that festivals that have managed to exist beyond the darned 7th year have a certain credibility.

* * *

TIP: At this stage of the distribution, I can only advise that you check the submission platforms at least once a week and send out your film. This doesn't even have to cost very much. Many of the smaller, but also larger festivals (especially in Europe) only charge small fees. And who knows, you might even get a fee waiver or two. The point now is to submit as much as your budget will allow. And as regularly as possible.

* * *

IMPORTANT! Besides, it is crucial in this phase to keep the film's status up to date on the submission platforms, the website and in the press kit. The information about which festivals it was or will be shown at greatly influences its future festival career.

* * *

49

THE FESTIVAL-SUBMISSION-SPREADSHEET

It's important to document when and where you submitted so you don't lose control of submissions and your finances. The best way to do this is to create the following columns in a simple Excel spreadsheet:

- Festival date
- Festival name and edition
- Website
- Submission fee
- Submission status

* * *

IMPORTANT! Unfortunately, you rarely get a message from festivals when your film has been rejected. But you can (and should) check the status on the submission platforms. There you can see clearly at which stage the film is in the respective festivals' selection processes. That is, whether a decision has already been made (selected or rejected) or not yet (pending).

* * *

50

THE SHOTGUN METHOD

Another popular submission method is to send the film everywhere, where it reasonably meets the festivals' requirements. The various filters offered by the submission platforms are particularly helpful for this. Especially the filter that makes it possible to get only festivals displayed that do not charge a fee or only a small fee with one click.

I am well aware that this method is very controversial. Film-makers often shy away from it because they fear that small festivals will dilute their film's festival vita. In other words, festivals listed in the press kit that are unknown could make an unprofessional impression on curators of larger festivals. Besides, many filmmakers do not see the point of submitting to festivals to which they will most likely not travel anyway and where there is little or no gain. On the other hand, film festivals are afraid of a flood of film submissions that only meet the criteria halfway or not at all.

Nevertheless, I am convinced that the so-called scattershot method, at the right time, can ultimately be good for the film as well as for the worldwide short film audience. However, there are a few things to take to heart:

• **The timing.** Please don't send your film around too early. As discussed in the previous chapters, it's relevant that you find a decent premiere first. After that, it is advisable to continue focusing on prestigious festivals. Whereas after the film's official release, you can start to spread the submissions a bit further (7th edition rule). Only after a certain period of time - sometime between 6 and 12 months after the premiere - it makes sense to really spread the film widely and submit it to unknown as well as very small or new festivals. In other words, If you want to pull out the shotgun, go for it. But it's best to do it six months to a full year after the premiere, depending on how long you want the film to be out.

• **Festival Vita.** I would include all festivals and awards in the film's vita. However, if you feel that the smaller festivals are drawing too much attention to themselves, for example, because they are so prevalent, then it is perfectly legitimate not to mention them at first. In this case, you only include a selection of festivals in the film vita, the press kit, the website and the submission platforms. However, this is a tightrope walk. It can also make quite an impression to have a long list of festival participation.

• **Festival Regulations.** Even if it costs little or nothing to submit to a festival, that doesn't mean you should mindlessly take advantage of it. Always make sure that your film complies with the festival regulations. Most of the time, the festivals where you can submit for free have a strong focus on certain themes, genres or niches.

51

DOES IT MAKE SENSE TO SUBMIT TO SMALL AND UNKNOWN FESTIVALS?

Yes, it makes sense. Period. Small and tiny film festivals can become a fantastic experience for filmmakers, and I can highly advise that you submit your film, after a while, there as well.

The fact that festivals are unknown is often simply because they haven't been around for that many years. But just because they were founded maybe fifty years after Oberhausen is no reason to devalue them across the board. On the contrary, it is often precisely at these small, personal festivals that genuinely enriching experiences arise.

Here, the organizers often make a particularly warm effort with the filmmakers. In most cases, you receive great hospitality, have the opportunity to meet other filmmakers in a very personal atmosphere, and get direct feedback on your film. The small festivals especially offer a great chance to get to know the country and its people, as they often provide sightseeing trips in small groups. Apart from that, you will have the chance to watch other short films in a very cosy atmosphere. And who knows, you might even win a prize in the end.

Some of these film festivals are real gems that may be yet undiscovered, but could certainly play a big role in the future. Many festivals have recently built up a considerable reputation in just a few years. It could be that the festival whose first or second edition you have just attended will also succeed in doing so.

Incidentally, many small festivals offer quite decent prize money. And the competition is naturally less than at larger ones. I was also often surprised at how many spectators were sometimes present at these festivals, which at first glance seemed so small. Some of these festivals even manage to fill larger movie theatres then their more prominent counterparts.

Moreover, you support these festivals through your submission. Provided, of course, you've made a good short film. Because unknown festivals have a much harder time getting great films and inspiring their quite fresh audience with short films.

So I hope I have convinced you. Please submit to the smaller festivals and visit them if you can somehow arrange it. I've had some of my most beautiful and moving experiences at those very festivals. And why should a certain audience be denied your film just because others don't think the festival is important enough that it's or too small? Primarily, you made your film to tell a story. Does it really matter so much where your audience is located?

* * *

TIP: If you feel that these very small and unknown festivals dilute the film's vita or seem too unprofessional, leave them out for now. Don't mention them at all, or not so prominently in the press kit and on the website, but still note them separately.

But don't be too hasty. Some experiences have shown me that this fear is often unfounded. On the contrary, in our agency we have mostly found that a longer film vita also increases the rate of acceptance.

However, you should make sure that only legitimate festivals adorn the vita and no fake ones!

52

WHAT ARE FAKE FESTIVALS AND HOW DO YOU AVOID THEM?

Thanks to digital submission platforms, it's pretty easy to set up a festival these days. However, this brings impostors and fraudsters alongside the advantages.

Unfortunately, and especially on the largest film platform FilmFreeway, there is little control over the claims of founders of new festivals. Many swindlers are charging submission fees for "festivals" that don't actually take place. Or are awarding submitted films without screening them and then demanding horrendous fees for sending the certificates or trophies.

Fortunately, however, these scammers are relatively easy to spot. Often a quick look at the festival website or the festival statutes on the submission platform is enough. I'll go into more detail about how to unmask these fake festivals in a moment.

But there are also a few more persistent comrades who operate in the grey area and are harder to identify. They host some kind of event that only remotely resembles a film festival, but their primary concern is to flush as much money as possible into their own pockets. For them it's unfortunately not about offering short films an appropriate platform.

For example, I just heard about a "festival" that operates in various European countries. The organizers arrange screenings, but they take place in hotel lobbies on the outskirts of big cities like London and are hardly ever visited. Filmmakers are sold high-priced hotel accommodations and offered tickets to overpriced gala events - where they then have to pay extra for every sip of wine. In short, the filmmakers are being fleeced.

Sure, these kinds of "festivals" offer the opportunity to collect selection laurels easily and usually relatively cheaply, but you should think twice before playing this game. With a submission, you support windy businesspeople and contribute to this frustrating development in the festival landscape. Moral concerns aside, there are economic reasons not to submit to these half-baked festivals. In the end, you're paying money for laurels that are of little use to you. It is now widely known that these pseudo-festivals exist and no one is impressed any more by the Official Selection Laurel of a festival that has just held its first or second edition, or isn't known at all.

So that you can better separate the wheat from the chaff, I've collected a few characteristics that indicate you might be dealing with a fake festival:

• **No public screenings.** If a festival doesn't offer public projections of films, all alarm bells should be ringing. Film festivals screen films in front of an audience. Period. If only gala events occur or the films are presented exclusively to a jury, it is not a film festival. Especially not if the filmmakers have to pay steep entrance fees for award dinners or the like. From this type of festival usually only the organizer benefits.

• **Suspicious festival name.** There are many pseudo-festivals that try to attract filmmakers' attention through their name in order to generate as many submissions as possible. Some use prestigious sounding cities in their title (such as The Madrid International Film Festival, Berlin Independent Film Festival or Stars Hollywood Festival). Others try to suggest national or even international prominence by dropping country names (such as The Alaska International Film Festival, California Film Awards or European Independent Film Awards). Here you have to be careful not to confuse these freeloaders with the well-known festivals in Madrid, Berlin, Los Angeles, Anchorage, Cannes, Toronto, Venice, etc. when submitting. A quick look at the website or a fast Google search will do.

• **This is the first time the festival is being held.** If you can't find anything online about past editions of the festival, it's probably the first edition. This doesn't have to mean anything bad because every festival is held for the first time at some point. But you should be very careful here, especially if you are asked to pay higher submission fees. Festivals that take place the first time and are serious about it don't ask for any or only for very low fees.

• **Several hidden costs.** A few black sheep among festivals give filmmakers an adventurous catalogue of quite expensive offers once their films have been selected. These can be, for example, advertising pages in the program booklet as well as award dinners, poster displays and tickets to the other screenings or even to their own film.

Sure, some festivals offer great workshops or masterclasses, for example, whose costs are justified. But the line between real festivals and ones that simply exploit filmmakers is quickly blurring. Please don't pay for pages in programs or to put up posters, and certainly don't pay to screen your own film. Legitimate festivals usually take care of those things free of cost.

• **Long Call for Entries.** If the festival puts out a call for film submissions throughout the whole year, there may be something fishy going on. Usually, film festivals can't afford to evaluate films year-round.

• **No website or mysterious, content-less websites.** A look at festival websites often speaks volumes. If a festival only has a simply designed alibi website that hardly reveals any information, then you should be careful, especially if the imprint and any contact information are missing. Usually, festivals like to present themselves online in detail. They introduce their team and publish information about the event.

Instead, typical fake festivals like to overload their website with stock photos of charming landscapes or striking buildings (Brandenburg Gate, Statue of Liberty, Eiffel Tower, etc.). Besides, there are often endless, confusing lists of categories for which awards are given. If there are any, the published texts often contain spelling and grammatical errors of all kinds. Information on screening times and locations is sought in vain. Just like information about the festival organizers, the jury members or the selection process.

• **Hardly any contact possibilities.** You should also take special care if there are not enough contact possibilities on the submission platform or website. At least one person, with their full name, should stand behind the festival and be easy to reach. Especially since an imprint (name, address, phone number and e-mail) is nowadays mandatory for any appropriate website.

• **High submission fees.** If a festival charges high submission fees, be wary, especially if it involves a new festival. High submission fees are only justified for festivals that have built a particular industry reputation over the years. For Cannes, you can pay a few euros more. But it makes no sense to throw such high fees down the throat of totally unknown festivals.

• **Countless awards are presented**. If a festival offers multiple awards, in a confusing number of categories and subcategories, the chance is high that something is wrong here. If you are then asked to pay large sums of money for the awards' shipping, then you know what the "festival" is mainly about.

• **There are no cash prizes to be won.** If the winner of a film festival only gets a PDF certificate sent by e-mail (or nothing at all), it might be the case that the money earned here mainly flows into the organizers' pockets.

• **The festival exists in several cities.** There are a few pseudo-festivals that take place under similar names in various cities around the world. They have names such as Madrid Independent Film Festival, Berlin Independent Film Festival and Stockholm Independent Film Festival. Mostly the same organizers are behind these pseudo-festivals. There are already a few groups, especially at FilmFreeway, who are skimming off the top here on a grand scale and with a method.

• **There is no detailed program.** If it is not possible to find out the festival's program, i.e. to find out which film will be shown when, then at some point the only conclusion is that there is none. And no program, in turn, means no festival.

• **The festival includes all submissions in its program.** If a festival advertises that it will include every film for which the submission fee has been paid, then you'd better not waste money here.

* * *

TIP: If you have doubts about a festival, do a quick Google search. Don't be blinded by great 5-star reviews on submission platforms which could well be written by friends or hired writers.

* * *

FOR MORE INFORMATION on fake or pseudo festivals, I can recommend shortfilm.de, especially the article "Laurels for Greenbacks – Making Money with Short Films in a Thriving Festival Scene." The article can be accessed, in German or English, here: https://www.shortfilm.de/en/lorbeeren-fuer-kohle-in-einer-bluehenden-festivallandschaft-mit-kurzfilmen-geld-verdienen/

53

WELCOME TO THE DIGITAL WORLD

These days, there are many ways to get yourself and your films noticed online. A website is now standard for serious filmmakers. And almost every filmmaker (and film) has a profile in the leading social networks. Besides, there are more and more ways to publish films online on free-access portals such as Vimeo, but also as part of video-on-demand platforms, such as Amazon.

Besides the many advantages that digital options bring, there are accompanying weak points and some faux pas you could commit. To make sure that doesn't happen to you, I'll talk about the different opportunities that the digital world offers you in the coming chapters.

54

THE PERFECT WEBSITE FOR YOUR FILM AND YOU

If curators like your film, they will look for you on the Internet. If producers like your film, they will search for you on the Internet. If viewers like your film, they will look you up on the Internet. I could go on with the list, but I think the message is clear: in the end, everyone will look for you on the Internet.

Therefore, the website is next to the film itself and the press kit, the most potent tool to promote your projects and you. For the best possible distribution of your work, it should be possible to find you under your artist name on the Internet. Ideally, people will be able to find and watch your current projects when they search for you.

A simple website with a short biography of the director, a few details about the making of the respective films, illustrated with film stills, is already enough to satisfy most searchers' curiosity. If you then indicate where the film was shown and what awards it could win, you already set yourself apart from many others. Unfortunately, very few filmmakers understand how useful a well-built website can be, let alone how to build and maintain a great one.

Yet these days, at least technically, it's become very easy. Even without any programming skills, you can create a professional-looking website with, for example, homepage building systems like Wix (www.wix.com) or Jimdo (www.jimdo.com). These user-friendly drag-and-drop solutions allow you to achieve very vivid results within a few hours. No previous experience is required.

However, if you have a little more time and patience, I would recommend you learn WordPress (www.wordpress.com), as you have much more flexibility and options here.

If you are afraid of any initiative in this matter, there is also the possibility of hiring a freelancer or a company. In this case, the website should be programmed in such a way that you can at least update it yourself afterwards.

The website, no matter how you create it, should contain at least the following information:

- A short and concise biography of you.
- Information about your previous projects (if any), such as a brief synopsis, a few strong film stills, and significant nominations and awards.
- Examples of your work. It's best to embed clips from films or trailers on the website. You should also prominently link your other online accounts, such as Vimeo, YouTube, Facebook, Instagram, Twitter, LinkedIn, etc.
- An easy way to contact you. Preferably via a simple contact form.
- The option of downloading press material (press kit,

film stills, photo of you, etc.) about your latest projects.

- The usual pages you need to create to be legally on the safe side (imprint, cookie notice, etc.).

Examples of a few plain but successful short film websites are:

The Curfew (Dir: Shawn Christensen): http://www. curfewfilm.com

The Neighbours Window (Dir: Marshall Curry): http://www.theneighborswindow.com

Toyland (Dir: Jochen Alexander Freydank): https://www. thunderroadfeature.com

The Phone Call (Dir: Mat Kirkby): https://thephonecallfilm.com

* * *

IMPORTANT! You should either set up your website so that it does not need regular updates, i.e. do without the news section and a blog. Or - and this is, of course, more promising - update it regularly. With information dated two years ago, a website is not a good advertisement; rather, it is the opposite.

55

WHAT SOCIAL NETWORKS SHOULD YOU USE?

Facebook, Instagram, Twitter and the like are all suitable for promoting your film and you as a filmmaker. Especially if you manage to gather a fan base around you, this can open many doors. Meanwhile, some festival organizers and sales agents also look at how many followers you or your film have.

But you don't have to do everything. I would advise you to focus on the network that you are most comfortable with. That's often an intuitive decision. But then you should be active there. For example, that means that you regularly post the successes of your films, such as festival participations or awards. Or announce your next projects. Besides, it is always appreciated in these networks if you share personal thoughts. If you also succeed in communicating added value for your readers, perfect. This could be, for instance, tips on filmmaking or sharing interesting articles you've come across. Maintain contact with other industry representatives there as well. Share their posts, congratulate them on their successes, or participate in discussions.

* * *

TIP: You can also promote your newsletter on your website and social networks. Through this newsletter, you can either send news about your current short film or let the readers participate in developing new projects. Again, it is very interesting if you also offer information in the newsletter that could help other filmmakers, such as tips and tricks on film production.

For newsletters of this kind, the service providers Mailchimp, CleverReach, Newsletter2go or ActiveCampaign are suitable. But be careful, there are different laws for e-mail marketing worldwide. In Europe, for example, you must use the double-opt-in procedure. This means that a subscriber must agree to be added to your e-mail list by clicking on a link in a separate e-mail.

In addition, there is a recent ban on tying in Europe. Accordingly, you must tell your e-mail subscribers what kind of information will be sent and at what frequency in advance. Besides, each of these e-mails must contain an imprint and the option to unsubscribe from the newsletter distribution list. So at this point, you must do a little research on the current legal situation.

* * *

56

SHOULD YOU RELEASE YOUR FILM ONLINE?

There are now countless ways to share your film online. Thousands of filmmakers have uploaded their work to platforms like Vimeo, promoted it on shortoftheweek.com, or sold it on video-on-demand services like Amazon. Only online do you have the unique and intriguing opportunity to engage with an audience of millions with just a few taps - an audience that is much bigger and more colourful than what you could ever reach through festivals.

So, yes, you should put your film online. It would be down-right careless to miss out on the opportunities that the Internet offers these days. Who knows, your film might even become the next viral super-hit. Or you might be discovered by key decision-makers. There are now a number of film-makers who have received promising offers because of their online success.

The much more exciting question is: Where do I publish my film online? And when?

57

WHERE CAN YOU PUBLISH YOUR SHORT FILM ONLINE?

The online market for short films is bigger than ever. There are now many serious streaming platforms continually looking for new content. So it's crucial to get an overview of the options before you release your film online.

In the following, I have listed a selection of the most interesting and most used platforms - without claiming it to be complete. It would be impossible to list all opportunities because new services appear daily, and others disappear again.

But if you know a provider that should be mentioned here, I would be pleased about an e-mail to contact@davidm-lorenz.com.

• **Vimeo (vimeo.com)**. Vimeo is the platform for high-quality short films. It has an enormous reach and millions of clicks per day. However, there is also a lot of competition. So you have to do a lot more than to upload your film. But I'll come back to that in a later chapter.

If you are lucky, your film might become a Staff Pick. This

means that Vimeo will highlight it as especially worth seeing. You can push this a bit by making the team behind the platform aware of your work's success so far (premieres@vimeo.com). A Vimeo Staff Pick is now a serious honour in the short film world.

Another helpful feature of Vimeo is the ability to block certain countries. So-called geoblocking can be very useful if, for example, you've made (or want to make) a deal with a TV channel that has demanded exclusive rights for a certain country. Or if you have already given the online rights for a country or continent to another platform.

• **Short of the Week (shortoftheweek.com)**. The creators behind this website have made it their goal to distribute high-quality short films. They do this with great passion and much success. However, the films shown here are curated. That means it's not entirely up to you whether your work gets published.

If you're interested in being featured on Short of the Week, you'll first have to send the creators a link to your short film and pay a small fee. What's really great here is that you'll always receive feedback and a detailed review of your film via e-mail. But don't get your hopes up. Since the program at Short of the Week is strictly curated, an acceptance here is already considered an award by now.

Also on this platform, it is possible to block your film for certain countries. Short of the Week can also be combined very well with a release on Vimeo.

• **Film Shortage (filmshortage.com).** Film Shortage is the little brother of Short of the Week and works similarly. Here, too, the short films are curated. Again, you have to pay a small submission fee (cheaper than Short of the Week). And here, too, you get quick feedback on the film in the form of a rating or review. Beyond that, however, Film Shortage still offers the possibility of crowdfunding campaigns. However, the reach is considerably smaller.

• **Films Short (filmsshort.com).** Films Short, as the name suggests, is also entirely focused on short films and functions similarly as Short of the Week and Film Shortage. However, submission is free here. There's also no guaranteed response in return. But every short film published is discussed and can be commented on by viewers. You can find - clearly arranged, divided into different categories - a variety of films on the website. Films Short, however, only accepts short films whose running time is less than 20 minutes.

• **No Budge (nobudge.com).** This platform also curates exquisite short films. A new film is released daily. Here you also have the chance to win a prize for the best short film, announced monthly. In addition, No Budge offers a screening for a select group of films in front of an audience in Brooklyn, followed by a Q&A session and an after-show party. You have a lot of influence over the framework here and can help decide how long your film should be available.

• **Reelhouse (reelhouse.com).** Reelhouse is an online video platform that allows you to publish your films yourself. You have full control over the conditions under which your film can be seen, where and by whom. And you have the opportunity to earn money by setting a rental or purchase fee. There are also several other appealing features, such as a crowdfunding function or the option to offer your film for sale before it has been shot. I find the developers' ideas extremely exciting, and the cooperation with Sundance also indicates that this platform has much potential. So it might be worth taking a look at it.

• **Short Film Connection (shortfilmconnection.com).**
Short Film Connection is a social network and closed
community for anyone who has anything to do with short
film. On the platform, you can register as a filmmaker,
festival or school. You will then have access to the profiles of
other users and the short films uploaded so far. Here you
have the opportunity to draw attention to yourself and your
film exclusively among industry representatives and to
establish contacts.

• **Netflix (Netflix.com).** I'm sure you know Netflix and I
don't need to say too many words about it. With this
premium subscription channel, viewers pay a monthly fee
and can access all movies on it. However, Netflix is not
exactly known for its selection of short films, but rather for
the feature films. Still, there are some short film gems
there. But it's not too easy, as you have to scroll through
some menus and scroll a lot beforehand. And it's not
exactly easy to place a short film on Netflix either since
direct submission is not possible. Netflix prefers to deal
with intermediaries. Usually, these are established distributors, sales agents or the so-called aggregators. This can
quickly become expensive, and Netflix also demands exclusivity in many cases. Besides, the technical quality requirements are quite high. Read more in the chapter "VoD: How
do I get my movie on iTunes, Netflix, Google Play or
Hulu?"

• **Sofy TV (sofy.tv).** Sofy TV is a streaming provider that
shows movies shorter than 40 minutes. With over a thousand
short films in its catalogue, the program offered here is now
quite extensive. According to the platform, over ten new
films are added every week. For a small monthly fee, viewers
can gain access to this pool of films. The creators' declared
goal is to trigger a short film revolution by enabling film-

makers to earn money with their short films. Now that's an endeavour worth supporting.

• **Shorts TV (shorts.tv).** Shorts TV says it has the world's largest portfolio of short films on offer and operates the "only 24/7 HDTV channel" dedicated exclusively to shorts. This apparently allows them to reach millions of households in the U.S., Europe and Africa. Again, it's strictly curated. If the program makers like your film, you'll be offered a contract for several years, though it won't yield any royalties for now. However, your work may be included in the illustrious circle of short films distributed via Shorts TV on other providers, such as iTunes. Then you'll earn money, too. The positive thing here is that this contract is not exclusive, so you have the opportunity to exploit the film elsewhere. Besides, you can submit without charge.

• **It's a Short (itsashort.com).** As the name suggests, the focus, also on this platform, is on short films. Viewers can get access to the full catalogue for a very small monthly fee. Every time your film is viewed, you earn money. Besides, you have the chance to win audience awards.

• **Facebook (facebook.com).** Here you also have the opportunity to upload your film. Since Facebook is the largest social network in the world, it is ideal for advertising. You can also embed your film via a link (for example via Vimeo), but Facebook's algorithms are set up so that directly uploaded content gets more attention. And that brings us to the most significant problem on Facebook. Everything you upload is subject to their algorithms. That means you have minimal control over who gets to see your project in their feed and who doesn't. These limited controls can be very frustrating.

• **Amazon Prime Video (amazon.com).** Between all the

feature films that Prime Video has to offer, there is also a fast-growing section dedicated to short films. The movies there fall under different subcategories, such as Award-Winning Short Films, Documentaries, Comedies, Mysteries & Thrillers, and so on. Amazon Prime has a similar reach and comparable name recognition as Netflix. And here, too, viewers can access a large pool of films for a monthly fee. For you as a filmmaker, however, there are significant differences. For example, Amazon Prime doesn't pay a one-time license fee; instead, you're paid based on the hours your films have been watched. Unlike Netflix, you can also submit on your own (via Prime Video Direct) and are not dependent on a middle man. This fact makes Amazon Prime very interesting for short films.

• **YouTube (youtube.com).** This video platform is undisputedly the largest and best known in the world. However, it is not exactly designed for high quality or artistically valuable short film productions. On the contrary, anyone can upload whatever they want here. And the viewers determine with their clicks where the trend goes (spoiler: mostly cat videos or make-up tips). High-quality short films rarely prevail here. But the exception proves the rule. For example, in recent years, there have been a few horror shorts and thrillers that have become viral mega-hits on YouTube, such as Don't Look Away by Christopher Cox and The Black Hole by Philip Samson and Olly Williams. And I also remember some excellent romantic comedies that got millions of views, like Signs by Stevey Mc Donald. Animated films are also particularly popular on YouTube. They set incredible viewership records, such as Dust Bodies by Beth Tomashek and Sam Wade, which has been viewed more than 60 million times.

* * *

IMPORTANT! It's better not to sign exclusive contracts with online providers. An exclusive contract means that the company you sign the contract with acquires the right to be the sole provider or seller of your movie. Especially if you give away the online rights exclusively, in the worst case worldwide, you deprive yourself of many opportunities.

Please sign shorter and non-exclusive contracts. Because then you would also have the option to release your film on different online platforms in parallel. At the end of the day, there is not much money in the short film industry, so most filmmakers care more about getting the film seen by as many people as possible. And an exclusive deal with a single distributor could prevent just that.

If you still want to sign exclusive deals, at least make sure they are not worldwide, but limited to certain countries.

* * *

UPDATE: Since the publication of this book, a lot has happened on the online marketplace for short films. I would like to express my sincere gratitude to all the readers who have sent me additional links and information. A special thanks goes to Michael Guerrini from Australia. Here is a brief update/extension of this chapter:

• **Indieflix (indieflix.com)**. A streaming platform purely for independent film of all formats, including short films. There is an opportunity for monetization.

• **Vidiverse (vidiverse.com).** Founded by Alex Proyas (director of "The Crow," "I, Robot," "Gods of Egypt"), Vidiverse is a streaming platform dedicated to the presentation and monetization of short films. Vidiverse combines SVOD

(Subscription Video on Demand) and TVOD (Transactional Video on Demand).

• **Argo Media (watchargo.com).** A popular, exclusively short film streaming platform with release and a great global notice. It offers a solid monetization system combining SVOD (Subscription Video on Demand) and AVOD (Advertising Video on Demand).

• **We Short (weshort.com).** A steadily growing streaming platform that exclusively showcases short films and originates from Italy. This platform offers a subscription-based monetization plan for short filmmakers, mainly from Europe but soon from around the world.

• **Selfmade – TV (selfmadetv.com).** A relatively new and continuously expanding streaming platform that primarily focuses on self-made, independent content, particularly short films.

• **Atlas Shorts (atlasshorts.com).** A streaming platform specialized in presenting short films in educational institutions worldwide. Once your work is selected by an educational institution, there is an opportunity for monetization.

Furthermore, these two film aggregators are highly innovative and promising:

• **Film Hub (filmhub.com).** Film Hub was developed by Klaus Badelt (film composer for "The Prince of Egypt," "Pirates of the Caribbean" films, "The Time Machine"). It is an aggregator website through which filmmakers can distribute their works and be forwarded to television stations worldwide, as well as various streaming services like Amazon Prime, Hulu, Apple TV, and Tubi TV. The fee is 20% of the earnings generated from views, and Film Hub provides users with analytics.

- **Altavod (altavod.com).** Altavod was launched by Robert Schwartzman. It is an aggregator channel where filmmakers can self-distribute and market their works. Altavod offers multiple marketing and distribution packages with only a 9% cut.

58

WHEN SHOULD YOU PUBLISH YOUR SHORT FILM ONLINE?

This question is not easy to answer, and this is where opinions differ. Until recently, the rule of thumb was that a film should be shown at festivals for about two years before it made sense to release it online in any way. This was because many festivals stopped considering those films that were already accessible online. Also, the online release was just not that interesting.

But things have changed drastically in recent years. More and more festivals are relaxing their rules and opening up to short films that can already be seen online. Recent surveys have shown that nowadays, almost two-thirds of all festivals include films in their program that have already been released online. Even prominent festivals such as Sundance are showing short films that are already available on Vimeo or YouTube. On top of that, online releases themselves are becoming more and more interesting. There are new options every day. So now you can even earn money from it and win prizes, while at the same time you have the chance to reach millions of people. In other words, releasing your short film online can open many doors for you.

So does it still make sense to spend more than two years hitting all the festivals and only go online afterwards? Probably not. Even some industry representatives, such as the makers behind Short of the Week, believe that an early online release doesn't harm the film, but rather does it good. And I've also experienced that most festivals' audience is very different from the audience that watches a film online. That's why I think it's no longer entirely appropriate for festivals to exclusively include short films in their programs that have not yet been viewed online.

But fortunately, it's not an either-or decision either. There is no longer one right way. The different types of distribution are not mutually exclusive; on the contrary, they overlap and fuel each other. Thus, the optimal distribution has become a balancing of interests and options.

You should accordingly ask yourself at each step what your goals are for your film and contrast the different options. Based on your goals, you can then decide what to focus on and when.

But there is still a kind of roadmap that I would like to recommend to you:

1. INTERNATIONAL PREMIERE
2. LARGER FESTIVALS
3. SELLING THE FILM (TV ETC.)
4. SMALLER FESTIVALS
5. SELLING THE FILM ONLINE
6. ONLINE FOR FREE

1. YEAR   2. YEAR   3. YEAR

In this graphic, I have tried to outline what an optimal film distribution can look like. In other words, a distribution that takes advantage of all the opportunities that are available for short films nowadays. A lot has already been discussed, but I'll try to summarize it briefly here.

Basically, I would advise every filmmaker to consider all the possibilities and then just vary the focus. In doing so, I still tend to look for one (or more) interesting festival premieres first. That means submitting only to the prestigious festivals for now, until you get an acceptance that has the potential to generate a lot of attention. And even after that, I wouldn't rush into anything, but first continue to submit to larger festivals, as explained earlier, that require country premieres, exclude online releases, or only accept films from the previous year. Meanwhile, you should travel to at least one of the film festivals and promote your film. Usually, after a few months or a year at the latest, you can make a good assessment of your film's potential. If it's successful, I would add another festival year. And I would also submit to smaller festivals.

At the same time, you should also try to sell the film, firstly to

TV stations. Ideally, you will have found a distributor or sales agent at a festival who can help you with this. More about this later.

After that (or in parallel), I would try to exhaust the possibilities of earning money online. First, in addition to TV stations, only publish on online platforms on which the films are not publicly accessible, but only for paying viewers. That would be the various video-on-demand providers. Here I would still advise you to be careful, especially not to give too many rights out of hand.

And only later, when the festival run is entering its final stages and most sales opportunities have been exhausted, would I move to offer the film through free online portals. If the film is outstanding and has great potential to be a hit online, it will be even then. So don't rush, go step by step and exhaust all possibilities.

59

SHOULD YOU EVEN MAKE YOUR SHORT FILM AVAILABLE ONLINE FOR FREE?

There's not much to be said against exploiting the many opportunities offered by the digital world. And the well-known platforms that make content available free of charge are still the ones with the widest reach.

However, as already explained, a few factors speak against taking this step too early. For example, I would advise not putting the film online free of cost until the other options, such as selling it to TV stations or video-on-demand providers, have been exhausted and most importantly, only after the most important steps in festival exploitation have been taken. As long as you're still submitting your short to prestigious or mid-sized festivals, I'd hold off on the free online release, as it simply makes the film less attractive to many festivals. And if you're still looking for a suitable festival premiere for your film, I definitely wouldn't put it online.

* * *

IMPORTANT! For online distribution, especially world-wide, you must own all the rights to your work. If you have permission to use a piece of music for the festival distribution, this does not mean that you may use it for online distribution. Therefore, it is necessary to obtain the consent of each copyright holder whose work appears in your film. This applies to actors and musicians, the script, camerawork, and artwork or trademarks that appear in your film, or locations that you were allowed to use. For documentaries, it is of course, vital that you have the consent of all the people featured.

Festivals may ignore rights issues, as they usually have a small audience and the chances of someone seeking an injunction after the screening are minimal. For online releases, however, it's a whole different story. There are law firms that are geared solely towards seeking copyright infringement online.

SELLING SHORT FILMS

Yes, it is also possible to sell your short film. There are not such huge markets as for a feature film, but there are some interesting options. Much is going on now, primarily online. If your film has the potential to attract a larger audience, you now have the chance to get back part of your investment, maybe even all of it. And if things go really well, there might even be something left over for you and your team. In the following chapters, I will go into the different possibilities that are available to you.

VOD: HOW DO YOU GET YOUR FILM INTO ITUNES, NETFLIX, GOOGLE PLAY OR HULU?

A few providers have established themselves in the video-on-demand space. The biggest are probably iTunes, Amazon Prime, Netflix, Google Play and Hulu. While these platforms focus on feature films and series, you can find a few short films there too. And it can be a great feeling to have your short film here in the program.

However, this is a lot more difficult than publishing a film on Vimeo or YouTube, because many filmmakers dream of being presented by these platforms. And there is a strong oversupply of content. So the VoD services have to make a selection from a massive pot of films. Unfortunately, to keep this from becoming an administrative nightmare, they don't sign contracts with individuals or small film productions. Instead, they negotiate and cooperate only with an elite group of "producers, lawyers, managers, literary agents, and entertainment executives." These middle men take the work of making a strong pre-selection away from the platforms. They also check to see if the films meet the technical requirements.

So if you want to get your short film into one of these portals, you'll have to rely on professional help. In the best case, you work with a production company or a distributor that cooperates with these platforms. More about this later.

If you don't succeed in doing so, you still have the option of using the paid service of a so-called aggregator. These companies, which are relatively new, offer to prepare your film according to the technical requirements and distribute it to the appropriate platforms. If your film generates revenue, they report and submit it to you. In short, an aggregator acts as a trusted intermediary between you and the VoD services. A few aggregators active in the short film space include BitMax, Quiver digital, FilmHub, Juice Digital, and Walla.

However, if you decide to go this route, you'll have to dig into your own pockets first. Submitting through an aggregator will cost you a few hundred dollars. The amount of the fee here varies from provider to provider. It also depends on whether the aggregators will share in the profit or not. There are three business models of these aggregators:

1.) The aggregator sees itself exclusively as a service provider. That means you pay a one-time flat rate in advance. Afterwards, however, you receive 100% of all revenues generated in the so-called backend.

For a short film you have to calculate with an amount of about 400.00 USD for the first VoD provider and about 100,00 USD for each further one, if you want to receive 100% of the payouts in the end.

* * *

IMPORTANT! You don't need an aggregator for Amazon.

You can do the submission yourself through Prime Video Direct. Don't get talked into a contract here.

* * *

2.) The aggregator sees itself as a service provider as well as a distribution company. In this case, you pay a fee in advance, which is usually lower than in the first example. However, the aggregator then also shares the revenue with you, to a percentage agreed upon before.

3.) The aggregator sees itself more as a distribution company. Then you will not have to pay a fee in advance. But in return, the aggregator will also get a significant share of the revenue. Moreover, before you get anything, the upfront expenses have to be covered first.

WHICH MODEL you choose depends on your financial situation, but also on your estimate of how high the payouts will be.

In any case, the film has to pass a strict, manual quality control. This is because the renowned VoD platforms are incredibly meticulous about the technical quality of their films.

So the submission process usually starts with you approaching an aggregator and presenting your film as best you can. The aggregator will then assess whether your film has a chance or not and offer you a contract accordingly. If you come together, you will receive a delivery guide that outlines the files needed for each platform and their specifications. This usually includes film stills, making-of photos, etc.

Once you have all these things together, you send them to the aggregator. There, your film is then subjected to a meticulous quality control and then forwarded to the VoD services, provided it has passed the check.

TIP: You may be daunted by the amount of money you have to pay upfront to submit your film. Therefore, I would like to point out that there are several free or low-cost options for positioning your film on alternative VoD platforms. I have listed some of these providers in the chapter "Where can I publish my short film online?"

* * *

62

HOW DO YOU MAKE YOUR SHORT FILM
AN ONLINE HIT?

How do you make your short film an online hit?
Nowadays, unfortunately, it's no longer enough to upload a film and then wait for the clicks. Self-runner, like there were in the early days of YouTube, which became mega-hits without any promotion, are history. Even if your masterpiece was a big festival hit, it doesn't necessarily mean that success will be repeated online. Vimeo and YouTube are just flooded with films. The competition is enormous, and it's not easy to stand out from the crowd these days. It now takes quite a bit of dedication to do so. Because in the meantime, just as in festival distribution, there is a direct correlation between effort and success online.

Once you've uploaded your film, be sure to start trumpeting the good news. Do some proper promotion on the social networks you're active on. Urge your friends and team members to share the link. In the best case, you can also get bigger influencers excited about your film and get them to share it. Also, contact film bloggers or other online editors who might be interested in recommending your film.

Perhaps it is based on a topic that could mobilize many supporters? If so, it's worth visiting the relevant forums or writing directly to the opinion leaders in the field. In other words, look for as many digital ways as possible to promote your film.

Also, try to be everywhere at the same time. One of the biggest misconceptions among short filmmakers is that the film should only be released on one platform to garner all the traffic there. That may have been true at one time, but it is no longer. Because nowadays, every major platform has algorithms that favour the so-called native videos instead of embedded links. Plus, they all cater to their own audiences. This means that you simply have very different audiences depending on whether you post on Vimeo, Facebook, YouTube, etc. Furthermore, someone else may publish your work. If your film is a hit on Vimeo, there's a good chance that someone else will upload it to YouTube for you. The more successful your film, the more tedious and time-consuming it will be to scour the Internet for these unauthorized copies. You can prevent this by publishing yourself in the appropriate networks. This way, you make sure that all the traffic ends up with you.

To get the best possible visibility, you should present your film on as many platforms as possible. There is little risk in doing this, as long as you own all the rights, don't upload too early, don't give away the rights exclusively, and don't enter into any contracts with dubious websites.

63

WHAT DOES A SALES AGENT OR SHORT FILM DISTRIBUTION DO?

First of all, a quick clarification of terms. Sales agent and distributor are two terms that are often confused. But the distinction is quite simple. A distributor takes care of a film's complete distribution, which usually includes festivals and other events where no or only a small screening fee is paid. On the other hand, a sales agent concentrates mainly on generating the highest possible sales with your film. The boundaries here are blurred, especially in the short film sector. The typical short film distribution is usually a hybrid of distributor and sales agent. He sends the film to festivals, but often only to a manageable number. Besides, he tries to sell the film to TV stations, streaming providers, hotels, museums, airlines, etc. In most cases, the distributors have gathered excellent contacts over the years and have found regular buyers.

Especially in Europe, some agencies have established themselves that focus on short films, as short films usually attract more interest from paying customers here.

Sometimes the distributor pays a fee for this in advance. The sums for this vary greatly and are somewhere between €500 and €5,000. But this is rather the exception. To get such offers, you'd probably have to win at least one major award or be nominated for an Oscar. Then several agencies would be interested in your film simultaneously, and there would be a bidding war.

Usually, however, the short film distributor will not advance you a fee but will give you a share of the revenue the film brings in. Your margin is usually between 50% and 75%.

However, you will usually be paid only after the distributor's expenses for your film have been paid off. These are the costs of making screening copies and promotional material.

* * *

IMPORTANT! You should agree with the distributor on an upper limit for such expenses so that you have a guarantee that these costs will not be too high. Otherwise, you won't have much left for yourself in the end.

* * *

ONCE THE CONTRACT IS SIGNED, you will need to send the distributor various screening copies and additional material. Especially when it comes to copyrights, you can expect the distributor to be stricter than festivals usually are. For example, you will most likely have to submit a music cue sheet that lists every music track that appears in your film. And you'll have to sign multiple times that you own all rights to the story and also have contracts with all other cast and crew members involved in the film. Once that is done, the distributor will do everything they can to sell the short film.

If the film is still at the beginning of its festival run, I would advise you to make an agreement with the distributor and stipulate that no sales will take place for the time being, which could jeopardize your festival strategy. Since it is usually in the distributor's best interest to have a film that celebrates festival success, they are very likely to agree to this.

* * *

IMPORTANT! However, it can also happen that agencies demand payment. Caution is advised here. Don't fall for a scam artist who then runs off with your money. Usually, a distribution agency does not ask for a fee in advance. So you have to be sure what you are paying for. Usually, the distribution then includes the festival market, as this is where the most money is spent. This means that the distributor submits the film to festivals for you. The higher the fees, the more extensively your film should be distributed.

If you want to go this route, you must research the providers' background. This means that you should take a look at the catalogue and preferably also contact filmmakers who are or were already under contract. You should then ask them for their opinion about the collaboration. In the best case, you should work with a provider that has been around for a few years and has already made a name for itself.

* * *

64

HOW DO YOU FIND A SALES AGENT FOR YOUR FILM?

I t is not easy to find a distributor or sales agent for your short film because there are not so many. There is also an oversupply of films. As a result, distributors only cherry-pick.

Most of the time, these agencies become aware of your film when it is shown at a prestigious festival. And especially if you win a prestigious award. Therefore, it can make sense to start your film's festival career with a festival that has a strong short film market attached to it. And which is attended by many industry representatives. Here, you have the highest chance that your film will be seen by a scout who will then offer you a contract. These contracts are usually limited in time, to an average of 3 years.

* * *

IMPORTANT! Many of these agencies insist on exclusivity. This means that you cannot sell your film elsewhere without consulting the distributor. However, there is usually a lot of room for negotiation as far as territories are concerned. Even though worldwide exclusivity is often asked for first, if possible, you should make a point of only signing contracts with agencies that are well established in the countries for which they demand exclusivity. This means, for example, that you entrust Spain and possibly Europe to a Spanish agency, but rather not the Asian market.

THERE ARE a few film festivals where gather a vast number of short film agencies. These would be, for instance:

- **Sundance Film Festival** (USA, January)
- **Clermont-Ferrand Int'l Short Film Festival** (France, February)
- **Berlinale – Berlin Int'l Film Festival** (Germany, February)
- **Tampere Film Festival** (Finnland, March)
- **Shortfest – Palm Springs Int'l Festival of Short Films** (USA, May)
- **Krakow Film Festival** (Poland, May/June)
- **Curtas Vila do Conde - Int'l Film Festival** (Portugal, July)
- **Edinburgh Int'l Film Festival** (UK, June)
- **TIFF – Toronto Int'l Film Festival** (Canada, September)
- **Encounters Film Festival** (UK, September)
- **Filmfest Hamburg** (Germany, October)
- **Kurzfilmtage Winterthur** (Switzerland, November)

Usually, festivals that have a market attached to them provide accredited attendees with some sort of overview showing who is present. In these lists, you can also see which distributors or sales agencies are on site. It would be best to write to them by e-mail or speak to them at the festival.

But even if your film did not make it into the catalogue of one of these festivals, you can try to contact a distributor. In that case, e-mail would probably be the method of choice.

That is, you write a short letter to the agency of your choice and introduce your new film. You should do as much advertising as possible. It's best to attach an informative press kit to the e-mail. Keep it as short as possible. And very importantly, include the streaming link to the film (password-protected) in the e-mail. If the press kit and cover letter are compelling enough, someone will watch your work. It's just a matter of time.

Very wellknown short film agencies are for example Premium Film (Paris, France), Feelsales (Madrid, Spain), Ouat Media (Toronto, Canada), interfilm Berlin (Berlin, Germany), Kurzfilm Agentur Hamburg (Hamburg, Germany) and New Europe Film Sales (Warsaw, Poland).

Before you contact them, you should have a look at their portfolio to see if your film fits in.

It can also be helpful if you can arouse a lot of interest. You should mention it if your film features a well-known actor or actress, if you have been invited to a renowned festival, if you have won an award or if the film deals with a current topic.

After that, it's a matter of waiting. Sometimes for a very long time. Your project will most likely end up in an endless list of films queued up for viewing by various agency staff. Don't get discouraged and don't get impatient if you don't get a response for several days or weeks. Only if you are still waiting for an answer to your January e-mail in March, may it be worthwhile to follow up again. Just write a short e-mail.

This should not sound too urgent or angry. It may only contain one sentence.

"Hey, just floating this to the top of the inbox – didn't want to get it to get buried, I realize you're busy."

This sentence, by the way, comes from Curt Jaimungal, who is behind indiefilmTO and gives helpful advice on independent filmmaking via his channel. Chances are if you use this in your e-mail, you'll get a response to it.

Incidentally, on the No Film School website, you'll find a very comprehensive list of international agencies currently distributing short films:

https://nofilmschool.com/2016/10/massive-list-international-distributors-your-short-film

Short film agencies are generally a great support in the commercial distribution of your film. They have a large pool of regular clients, depending on how established they are. Besides, many TV channels or other platforms prefer to negotiate with distributors because they have already made a strict pre-selection and the rights have been cleared. Besides, larger customers like to buy packages with several short films. In the best case, the agencies are also in good contact with the important festivals and advertise their current catalogue with them.

So if a distributor approaches you, I would advise you to consider cooperation. But even then, don't develop too high expectations. Just because an agency has shown interest doesn't mean that the film will become a worldwide hit.

If none of the agencies are interested in your film, it doesn't mean that much. In that case, like 99% of all short filmmakers, you'll have to take care of your film yourself. But now that you've read this book, that shouldn't be too hard for you, I hope.

CLOSING WORDS

Now it's time for closing remarks because you have reached the end of this book. First of all, I would like to thank you very much for reading through it. I hope I was able to give you some vital information and inspiration along the way.

Now it's up to you what you do with it. I would be happy if you implement some of it and achieve your goals. In any case, I'm keeping my fingers crossed that you find many viewers and that you succeed in inspiring people around the world with your short film.

If this book has helped you and added value in any way, I would love a 5-star review on Amazon!

If you have any questions, requests, complaints, or suggestions about the book or anything else you want to get off your chest, please feel free to contact me. I'm always open to criticism and new ideas and happy to help (contact@davidmlorenz.com).

Thanks again for reading this. I wish you a successful film distribution!

Made in the USA
Las Vegas, NV
06 April 2024